12/14

ARTISAN PIZZA
AND FLATBREAD
in Five Minutes a Day

ALSO BY JEFF HERTZBERG, M.D., AND ZOË FRANÇOIS

Artisan Bread in Five Minutes a Day:
The Discovery That Revolutionizes Home Baking

Healthy Bread in Five Minutes a Day: 100 New Recipes Featuring
Whole Grains, Fruits, Vegetables, and Gluten-Free Ingredients

ARTISAN PIZZA
AND FLATBREAD
in Five Minutes a Day

JEFF HERTZBERG, M.D., and ZOË FRANÇOIS

Photography by MARK LUINENBURG

THOMAS DUNNE BOOKS
ST. MARTIN'S PRESS 🍃 NEW YORK

THOMAS DUNNE BOOKS.
An imprint of St. Martin's Press.

www.thomasdunnebooks.com
www.stmartins.com

Design by Phil Mazzone

Photography copyright © 2012 by Mark Luinenburg

Library of Congress Cataloging-in-Publication Data

Hertzberg, Jeff.
    Artisan pizza and flatbread in five minutes a day / Jeff Hertzberg and Zoë François ; photography by Mark Luinenburg.
        p. cm.
    ISBN 978-0-312-64994-4
    1. Pizza. 2. Bread. 3. Cookbooks. I. François, Zoë. II. Title.
    TX770.P58H47 2011
    641.8'248—dc23
                                                                    2011026059

First Edition: November 2011

10 9 8 7 6 5 4 3 2 1

In memory of our first editor, Ruth Cavin (1918–2011), who took a chance on us and our cookbook idea. Her love of good food inspires us still.

To my mom, who always seemed to have fresh bread in our house.

—JEFF

To my dad, who taught me to live life with a sense of curiosity and adventure.

—ZOË

CONTENTS

ACKNOWLEDGMENTS

Our spouses, Laura Silver and Graham François, grinned and bore it, eating pizza at least three times a week (it's a tough job but someone has to do it). Laura still edits everything before it goes out the door, and Graham keeps our design and incredible Web site up to date.

Recipe-testers became friends, and friends became recipe-testers, recipe-inventors, and other helpers. Thanks to Leslie Bazzett, Jay, Tracey, Gavin, and Megan Berkowitz, Sarah Berkowitz, Betsy Carey, Marion and John Callahan, Barb Davis, Fran Davis, Shelly Fling, Beth Fouhy, Anna and Ewart François, Leslie Held, Lisa Hoff, Kathy Hoff, David Hughes, Allison Jensen, Kathy Kosnoff and Lyonel Norris, Kelly Lainsbury, Tefera Landis, Alec Neal, Barbara and Kristin Neal, Carey Neal and Heather Pamula, Craig and Patricia Neal, Lorraine Neal, Peggy Orenstein, Elaina and Paul Perleberg, the staff at Quang, Danny Sager and Brian McCarthy, the Schmitt family, Sally Simmons and David Van De Sande, Jen Sommerness, Sue and Eric Strobel, Debora Villa and Ralph Gualtieri, Lindy Wolverton, and Warren Zacher.

At St. Martin's Press, thanks to Peter Wolverton, Monica Katz, Matthew Baldacci, Amelie Littell, and Anne Bensson; thanks also to Leah Stewart, our terrific copyeditor, and Judy Hunt, who created another great index. Our agent-team of Jane Dystel, Miriam Goderich, and Lauren Abramo was brilliant as always. Jeff Lin of BustOutSolutions.com created our new mobile Web site version.

Gratitude to colleagues in our baking and culinary worlds past and present: Brett Bannon at Bret's Table, Karl Benson and all of the wonderful folks at Cooks of Crocus Hill, Chris Bianco of Pizzeria Bianco, Steven Brown of Tilia, Jennifer Burkholder, the kind people at Dunn Bros, Stephen Durfee of the Culinary Institute of America, Barbara Fenzl of Les Gourmettes Cooking School, the generous bakers at Taste of India for teaching us how to use a tandoor oven, Michelle Gayer of Salty Tart, Thomas Gumpel of Panera, Bill Hanes, Chopper Bitterman, Kelly Olson, and Sherie Wood of Red Star Yeast, Patrick Lobo and Tara Steffen of Emile Henry, Tom Payne, P. J. Hamel, and Michael Bittle of King Arthur Flour, Stephanie Jameson and the crew at The Chef's Gallery, Brenda Langton of Spoonriver, Michael London of Max's, Ray Loomis from Mohawk Valley Trading Company, Rudy Maxa, Dan "Klecko" McGleno of St. Agnes Bread Company, Riad Nasr of Minetta Tavern, Serap Oligney and her sister Fatos of Depot 62, John Puckett and John Soranno of Punch Pizza, Peter Reinhart, Suvir Saran, and Charlie Burd of American Masala, and Andrew Zimmern, Dusti Kugler, and Molly Mogren of Food Works.

Our photographer, Mark Luinenburg, continues to be a great friend and creative force behind the look of this book. We worried that a bunch of round flat things wouldn't be all that interesting visually. But just look.

And again, our families did a superlative job supporting us in this most unusual adventure: Zoë's husband, Graham, and her two boys, Henri and Charlie, and Jeff's wife, Laura, and his girls, Rachel and Julia.

THE SECRET

The "Secret" works especially well for pizza and flatbread: Mix enough dough for many pizzas or flatbreads and store it in the refrigerator.

Pizza and flatbreads were by far the fastest breads in our first two books, and everyone loves pizza. They're fast because they don't require resting and rising time after shaping, the way loaf breads do. You can have fresh-baked flatbread with tonight's dinner in the time it takes you to take dough from the fridge, roll it out, and slip it into the oven. Active time, as always, is less than five minutes a day. How's the trick done? First, mix enough dough for many pizzas or flatbreads in a container, and let it sit for two hours (or no time at all for the non-yeasted doughs on pages 99–104). Now take a piece of dough, roll it out, and bake a pizza or flatbread—in most cases no further resting or rising is necessary. Refrigerate the leftover dough for use over the next five to fourteen days (the dough will develop richer flavor over its storage life). The baking time is ten minutes or less for thin pizzas, pitas, and flatbreads, and a little longer for focaccia. You will be a kitchen hero!

INTRODUCTION

Lunch with Jeff and Zoë

"Jeff and Zoë have an ideal friendship: They share an obsession with food, and they've managed to turn it into their work. I should know, because I've spent the better part of the last eight years slipping around my kitchen floor like a pizza pie on a floury paddle (Jeff is my husband). I sat down for lunch with Jeff and Zoë recently and they started talking about their favorite subject: pizza." —Laura Silver

L: Is either of you willing to claim a favorite pizza?
Jeff: I love them all, but especially anything with roasted red peppers and eggplant—something caramelizes in the skin and transforms the flavors.
Zoë: I have to say the Turkish lamb pizza. You sprinkle the spiced meat with parsley and onions and squeeze lemon over it and then roll it up like a crepe. It's unlike any pizza I've had and it's fun to eat.
L: Is there one particular place you can find the best pizza, do you think?

Zoë: Naples.

L: That was a quick answer.

Zoë: The pizza was incredible.

L: And why was that?

Zoë: Well, for one thing, the setting is so dramatic. And it's *their* food. Pizza is what the people actually eat. We went to a restaurant that had nothing on the menu but two pizzas: *Margherita* (tomato, basil, and mozzarella) and *marinara* (tomato, no cheese). That was the whole menu, and there were lines out the door. It's a $2.50 meal. The crust was delicate and really salty, which I love.

L: How about you, Jeff? Where do you think you can find the best pizza?

Jeff: I wish I could say it was a pizza joint near where I grew up in New York, but . . .

L: But that wasn't such great pizza, was it?

Jeff: No, it wasn't. But I worked there, delivering pizzas in high school, so it's my sentimental favorite. I loved what Zoë said about the setting—and the memory of the time and place. I don't even know if we really remember the flavor of food we ate years later. Food is so wrapped up in what you're doing, who you're with, what you're drinking—the whole experience, not just the direct effect on your taste buds.

Zoë: That's right, setting is everything. In Naples there are laws about how these pizzas are made, but they didn't taste the same from one restaurant to the next—even though they had these crazy guidelines that they had to follow. So the chef, the oven, the weather, the people you are with—they all make a difference.

Jeff: I'm not entirely convinced that Italy's pizza is better than American. I haven't been to Italy in twenty years but we had pizza in Rome that we thought was great. I remember the setting, I remember walking around with it, I remember being with Laura, but do I remember what it tasted like? I have no idea—until I go back, all I can tell you is that American pizza has become world-class.

Zoë: When I was a kid we'd visit New York City and get Ray's (there's one on every corner) and I absolutely loved that style—dripping with cheese, and soft, with a fluffy crust. I really love almost all pizza.

Jeff: So do I!

Zoë: That's why this is a perfect book for me—I've gotten to eat pizza three times a day.

Jeff: What I love about pizza is that it doesn't have to be taken seriously. It's not a serious person's food.

L: Talk about how you collaborate. Do you each develop recipes separately?

Jeff: Yes and no. We're in touch constantly and coordinate our recipes as they develop, and then we get together at the coffee shop to sample our creations, critique them.

Zoë: We give each other criticism and encouragement. And more criticism. We're a good pair because we bring very different things to the table, literally.

L: What do you each bring?

Zoë: Jeff came up with the five-minutes-a-day concept and he was not confined by the rules of being a chef: the techniques and the traditions around how things "are done." So he has no qualms about doing things—or not doing things—his own way, and the results are delicious. Working with Jeff now, I tend to think outside of that particular box—the professional's box. He also brings a calendar and spreadsheets. (Those are not my strongest skills.) And a sense of humor!

Jeff: Zoë brought professionalism to our books—a sense of artistry and careful attention to detail. She's had to produce dishes in the restaurant that come out the same every day—yet there has to be this harmony in the menu and a sense of coordination with the rest of the meal. Maybe most importantly, Zoë brought dessert to our books—I couldn't have imagined translating this method to brioche and other desserts.

Zoë: The fact that this method works with brioche proves how versatile it is.

Jeff: The truth is that I wanted to work with her because she's one of the nicest

---

people I've ever met. But nice as she was, I was sure her stuff wouldn't work—I was skeptical about that brioche.

Zoë: That's funny, I was pretty sure yours wouldn't work either. Good thing we were both wrong.

L: How many years have you been partners in this project?

Zoë: Eight years.

Jeff: We can laugh about this now, but I really had a hard time convincing her to try the method.

Zoë: Hounding is more like it.

Jeff: That's true. I started hounding her right after I found out she was a pastry chef. As soon as we started spending time with the kids at the museum, I told her The Secret (see page xiii). It was a great opportunity, and I knew it would be fun to work together.

Zoë: The first thing I tried baking was the original recipe—for bread—and I was completely blown away. I mean, it shouldn't have worked, based on what I learned in culinary school. I was excited for Jeff to do a book, but I only became convinced to do it *with* him when he made me a pizza. I knew if people found out about this, they would bake at home all the time. And we had to add brioche and lots of sweets.

Jeff: That was your precondition.

Zoë: Yes, but it was the versatility of the method that really excited me. It wasn't just that I could reproduce this one beautiful loaf of bread over and over again; it was that this bucket of dough could make this beautiful loaf, and this amazing pizza, and dessert.

Jeff: I have to admit I was pretty happy the day you tried the pizza and liked it. Speaking of pizza, our lunch is ready.

Zoë: Let's eat!

1

PIZZA AND FLATBREAD ARE THE FASTEST BREADS WE MAKE: STORING THE DOUGH MAKES THE DIFFERENCE

By the time we finished our second bread cookbook, we came to a basic truth: our pizzas and flatbreads were the fastest and often the most beloved recipes in our repertoire. Why? Because unlike loaf breads, they require little or no rest time after shaping them. So if you have a batch of our stored dough in the fridge (where it's been developing richer flavor over its storage life), and you've preheated your oven, you can be as little as ten minutes away from piping hot pizza, or even less for fresh pita flatbread. For busy people, there is no quicker dinner—as always, active time is under five minutes a day, because you spread the preparation time for your premixed dough over many pizzas and flatbreads.

We've included soups, dips, and spreads that turn flatbreads or pizzas into a complete and speedy meal. Ingredients will include grains and toppings from around the world, as well as healthier alternatives where possible. So this book can become the basis for entire meals that are perfect for busy households.

New pizzerias are popping up all over the United States, and pizza remains the nation's number one purchased meal. Despite this, there aren't many pizza cookbooks on the market today. And most recipes rely on dough that yields just one precious pie—not an option for most busy people. We have a voracious appetite for pizza, and so do our readers (that's what they told us on our Web site). Making your own pizza is much easier than it looks, and the options for toppings and crust mean that there's a world of variety. As in all our books, **the secret to baking it fresh every day is that the dough is on hand, *in your refrigerator,* all the time.** Storing the dough makes all the difference. Since you only mix once, but bake up to eight pizzas or flatbreads over a couple of weeks, you divide the prep time over all the pizzas and flatbreads you make from the batch.

Whether you're an old hand at baking or a novice, our helpful tips will let you perfect your pies. We start with basics in Chapter 2 (Ingredients), Chapter 3 (Equipment), and Chapter 4 (Tips and Techniques). And then you can start baking exquisite pies with our Master Recipe (Chapter 5).

2

INGREDIENTS

Making pizza and flatbread is a lot like baking regular bread, only quicker and flatter. Many of the ingredients are the same as in our first two books, but we discovered some new ingredients that will help you create world-class pizza and flatbreads. See Sources (page 281) to locate harder-to-find ingredients through mail order or the Internet.

Flours

Flours vary in important ways, and we've found that the most predictable results are obtained when you use standard supermarket flours. That's what we used to test our recipes. One way that flours vary (especially white flours) is in their protein content. Wheat protein is mostly gluten, a long, stringy molecule that gives dough its stretchiness and allows it to trap gas and rise. Let's talk about the flours we use in the book to make great pizza and flatbread.

Unbleached all-purpose white flour: In the United States, supermarket brands of unbleached all-purpose flour have a protein content of 10 to 11.7 percent, and that's what we used to test our recipes that call for unbleached all-purpose. Most of the protein in wheat flour is gluten, the resilient protein that gives bread dough its stretch and its ability to trap gas. Without it, bread and pizza would be way too dense. In Italian-style pizza, you need some gluten, but not too much—classic, thin-crusted pizzas are made with a lower-protein flour (see Italian-style "00" flour on page 5). Unbleached all-purpose is a nice compromise for most home pizza bakers. It's a typical ingredient that almost everyone has at home, and the protein content is at a medium level.

     If a recipe calls for *unbleached,* don't substitute bleached all-purpose flour. Bleaching removes some of the protein, and that throws off our recipes because protein absorbs water. When shopping, be careful, because most bleached flours don't label themselves prominently and if you don't search for the word "bleached," you may not find it. If you use bleached flour when unbleached all-purpose was called for, your dough will be too wet.

Bleached all-purpose flour: If you want to use bleached flour, use it in the recipe we created specifically for lower-protein flour (page 71); it makes a good substitute for low-protein, Italian-style flours like "00." As above, don't substitute it for unbleached all-purpose or the result will be too wet and difficult to handle.

Cake flour: Cake flour, being bleached and having a very low protein level, makes tender cake and desserts. This very low protein flour would not create enough structure to make a good bread or pizza, but when combined with unbleached all-purpose flour, it becomes a decent alternative to "00" Italian flour in classic Neapolitan pizza (page 73).

Gluten-free flours: Our gluten-free doughs use a variety of flours, such as brown rice, tapioca, teff, and white rice (sometimes labeled "sweet white rice flour").

The lack of gluten in these flours means that you have to add xanthan gum to the dough to give it the stretch and structure dough needs to be used as pizzas and flatbreads. Most of our recipes can use the gluten-free doughs, but you may need to refer to page 104 for specific rolling instructions.

Italian-style "00" flour (page 73): In Italy, low-protein "00" flour is the standard in thin-crusted, crisp-yet-tender Neapolitan pizza, but it's nearly impossible to find in U.S. supermarkets—"00" is an Italian designation. Technically speaking, "00" refers to the fineness of the grind ("00" is the finest), not the protein content. That said, Italian "00" is usually made from "soft" (low-protein) wheat, and it's the lower protein that makes for a tender (not tough) crust that crisps beautifully. In Italy, Neapolitan pizza (see page 73) is made from low-protein "00," with a little high-protein flour thrown in to provide some stretch. You can purchase Italian-style flour online; there are two sources in the United States. An Italian import, **Caputo "00" Flour**, is available through Amazon.com, and

> ∽
>
> **PROTEIN PERCENTAGES ARE REPORTED DIFFERENTLY IN THE UNITED STATES AND ITALY:** One area of confusion is that U.S. flour companies report protein content differently than Italian ones (the U.S. number is always lower). Don't be thrown by this if you try an imported flour—low protein Italian "00" flour is often reported with a protein percentage that makes it look like American all-purpose—but it's not; that's just a different way of measuring it.

King Arthur makes a domestic approximation with about the same protein level (about 8 percent), sold as **King Arthur Italian-Style Flour**. But be careful with labeling: King Arthur also makes a flour called **Perfect Pizza Blend**, but it can't be swapped into the "Crisp Yet Tender" recipe (page 71). At 11.1 percent,

Visit PizzaIn5.com, where you'll find recipes, photos, videos, and instructional material. See page 53 for outdoor grill instructions.

it's higher in protein than typical supermarket unbleached all-purpose flour. See **Pizza Dough for Throwing** (page 75) if you're interested in chewier crusts made from higher-protein flour.

You can approximate the low-protein effect of "00" flour with bleached all-purpose (page 71).

Bread flour: Typical U.S. bread flour is about 12 percent protein, and as in all-purpose flour, the protein is mostly gluten—and protein absorbs water. So, you need to increase the liquids if you substitute bread flour for all-purpose in our recipes (about a quarter-cup to one-half cup in the Master Recipe on page 59). Though dough made from bread flour takes longer to stretch, if you're patient with it, you get a gorgeous American-style pizza—a little chewier than its Italian cousin.

∾

THE HIGHEST-PROTEIN CONSUMER FLOUR IN THE U.S. IS KING ARTHUR HIGH-GLUTEN FLOUR, with 14.2 percent protein. That's considerably more than typical supermarket bread flours, so if you use it, you need to increase liquids in the recipe by one-half cup if you're swapping it for ordinary all-purpose (one-quarter cup if you're swapping it for ordinary bread flour). Their regular bread flour (12.7 percent protein) isn't much different from typical U.S. bread flours and can be interchanged with them.

Rye flour: Rye, in combination with white flour, makes a terrific rustic pizza or flatbread crust. Assuming that you will leave out caraway seeds, no one will recognize it as a cousin of deli rye bread (though if you top a rye pita with caraway, you'll have wickedly good deli-rye pocket bread, see Variation: Pita, page 201). Most rye flour that's readily available in the United States is very high in rye bran and really could be labeled as whole grain flour. The two products available in most U.S. supermarkets are Bob's Red Mill and Hodgson Mill, and both work nicely in our rye recipes. Interestingly, the packaging on those two products doesn't stress that the contents are whole grain—but they are. Exceptions are rye flours labeled as "light rye" or "medium rye," which are lower in bran and available from King Arthur Flour (see Sources, page 281). Since our Rustic and Hearty Rye Dough recipe (page 93) uses a relatively low proportion of rye flour, we found that it didn't make much difference whether we used whole grain rye, medium, or light. Though they produce slightly different consistencies, they all worked well. Use the whole grain rye products if you're interested in the health benefits of whole grain.

Semolina flour: Semolina is a high-protein wheat variety that lends rich yellow color and sweet flavor to Italian baked specialties. The best semolina is labeled as "durum flour." It's more challenging to find than typical flours, but Bob's Red Mill and King Arthur flour make nice products (see Sources, page 281). If you use flour labeled as "semolina" (commonly found in South Asian groceries), you'll find that it's usually a coarser grind and needs to be decreased in the recipes or the result can be an overly dry dough. We don't often see semolina used in pizza, but we think it's fantastic (page 80).

Spelt flour: We fell in love with spelt flour, a variety of wheat, while writing *Healthy Bread in Five Minutes a Day*. It's lower in gluten than ordinary wheat, which appealed to readers who were avoiding higher-gluten products (but spelt *cannot* be eaten, not even a little, by people with celiac disease). Whole grain spelt imparts a terrific mildly sweet flavor that appeals to kids who are wary of whole grain breads. Most of the spelt flour sold in the United States is whole grain, but there are some lesser-known varieties labeled as "light spelt"; they are lower in bran and absorb less water. Do not use them without adjusting the water downward, or the dough will be too loose.

Visit PizzaIn5.com, where you'll find recipes, photos, videos, and instructional material. See page 53 for outdoor grill instructions.

Cornmeal: We use cornmeal in several doughs for its wonderful earthy flavor and lovely crunch. Either white or yellow cornmeal can be used; other than the color, we didn't taste any difference. In the United States, cornmeal is often used under pizzas to help slide them off the pizza peel and onto the hot stone. In Italy, it's traditional to use white flour for that purpose. Either works well, but there are differences. Cornmeal can make more of a mess in the oven, with stray corn scorching and smoking on the stone or on the bottom of the oven. We tend to use flour on the peel to avoid these problems. This is especially true for pita bread—it's traditional to use nothing but flour.

Organic flours: We like to use organic flour when it's available; many of our readers tell us that the reason they started baking at home was because it was the only way to get affordable organic bread. There are now a number of organic flour brands available in the supermarket, but the best selection is still at your local organic food co-op.

Toppings

Don't overdo it with the toppings, especially with thin-crusted pizzas; lightly topped pies develop crisper crusts and are easier to slide off the pizza peel. The most visually impressive tomato and cheese pizzas are made with widely spaced chunks of cheese that allow the red tomato to shine through.

TOMATO AND TOMATO SAUCES

Fresh tomatoes: If you have summer tomatoes, especially home-grown, you owe it to yourself to use them on pizza. Slice or dice the tomatoes, get rid of some of the liquid by draining, reducing on the stove, or seeding them, and you have the world's finest pizza topping (see Tomato Toppings, page 109).

Canned tomatoes: You can use diced tomatoes, or whole ones pulsed in the food processor. In either case, decrease the liquid by pressing in a strainer (or reduce them in a saucepan). Otherwise, you can end up with a soggy crust. Crushed or pureed canned tomatoes also work nicely and, if not too liquidy, there is no need for straining or reducing. If diced tomatoes are too chunky for you, consider chopping them in a food processor, or even just mincing them on a cutting board with a knife.

Pizza sauce: Some people prefer a smooth sauce over chunkier options. Our recipe for smooth tomato pizza sauce can be made with canned tomato sauce, or crushed, diced, or whole canned tomatoes that have been processed with an immersion blender, food processor, or standing blender.

Basil: The bright summery taste of fresh basil is a knockout on homemade pizza. The dried herb isn't nearly as flavorful (some people find dried oregano to be more interesting than dried basil—so try a little of that if you don't have fresh basil in the house). In Italy, it's traditional to lay whole basil leaves on the pizza, but if you want the basil flavor to be well distributed across the pizza, you can break up the leaves into smaller pieces. Some professionals like to tear basil by hand to prevent discoloration. We've found that if you sliver or snip the herbs right before putting it on the pizza, there's minimal discoloration, and the flavor's terrific either way. Some *pizzaioli (pete-see-ó-lee)*, the men and women who make pizza, put

CHIFFONADE THAT BASIL? If you decide to cut fresh basil leaves for pizza, the quickest way to do it is to use the *chiffonade technique*. Stack four or five basil leaves, roll them into a tight cylinder, and quickly cut thin slices across the cylinder, starting at one end and working your way along. You'll end up with evenly cut ribbons that look great on pizza.

Visit PizzaIn5.com, where you'll find recipes, photos, videos, and instructional material. See page 53 for outdoor grill instructions.

the basil on *after* baking so that it just barely wilts, and retains its vibrant color and flavor. That's a matter of taste, so go ahead and try it both ways and see which you prefer.

In case you're keeping score, Italian law specifies whole basil leaves on Neapolitan pizza (see page 59) but does not absolutely prohibit slivered, snipped, or torn ones. Whew.

Cheeses

When using cheese on pizza, remember that the quantities in our recipe are only an approximation. Depending on the size of the pizza you are making, you will need more (or less) cheese than we specify. We tend to use less cheese than is typical for American-style pizza—we prefer the Italian style, which is usually built on a thin crust. Plus, using less topping works better with our dough, which has lots of moisture to begin with—too much cheese (or any topping) can prevent the crust from crisping. With pizza, sometimes less is more.

If you love pizza with extra cheese, you can do it, but don't make the crust quite so thin—try a quarter-inch thickness.

MEDIUM-SOFT CHEESES

With the exception of blue cheeses, medium-soft cheeses are generally interchangeable in our recipes. In most cases, if a pizza works with mozzarella, it will probably taste great with any other medium-soft cheese, and those subtle flavor changes are the spice of life—or at least, of pizza.

Mozzarella: Mozzarella is mild tasting but marvelous. You have three options for this most standard of pizza cheeses: commercial packaged mozzarella, or two kinds of fresh mozzarella, both of which tend to be more expensive than the commercial stuff. Let's talk commercial first—this is what most of us grew up on. It's drier than fresh mozzarella, and comes either as a block, or pre-shredded and tossed with starch to prevent the cheese from sticking together. Whole-milk or part-skim versions are available, and if you see "low-moisture," that's a good (but not essential) option (lower moisture helps pizza crusts stay crisp).

Once you've tried fresh mozzarella, you're bound to fall in love with it. You'll see what we mean once you taste it—people describe a "grassy" fresh dairy flavor, so try to imagine the sweet grasses that cows munch to fuel all that milk (OK, we don't really do that). Two kinds of fresh mozzarella may be available in your supermarket, so check before trying a specialty cheese store:

- **Cow's milk fresh mozzarella:** Mozzarella labeled as "fresh" is brighter white and has a creamy lightness. It's packed in whey or vacuum-packed in plastic (which excludes the whey). It has less moisture than *mozzarella di bufala*, which makes it a bit easier to work with (though it definitely has more moisture than commercial).
- ***Mozzarella di bufala*:** This very authentic mozzarella made from the milk of Italian water buffaloes is absolutely delicious, though it doesn't come cheap (someone really has to milk that water buffalo!). Be careful again when you put it on the pizza—**use it sparingly** because it is high in moisture—as the cheese melts, liquid seeps out and can soften the crust. Some of the great American pizzerias have rejected buffalo mozzarella because of this excess moisture, but we

Visit PizzaIn5.com, where you'll find recipes, photos, videos, and instructional material. See page 53 for outdoor grill instructions.

think it's fantastic when used carefully—use about 25 percent less *mozzarella di bufala* than you would with ordinary fresh or commercial mozzarella. In Italy, *mozzarella di bufala* is required only on the deluxe version of the authentic Naples-style pizza, known as *Pizza Napoletana Margherita Extra*. See what you think.

Asiago: In Italy, *asiago* is a bit of a cheese chameleon—a wide range of varieties are available there, all produced in the Italian Alps. Dry-aged versions are reminiscent of crumbly and sharp Parmigiano-Reggiano, but the fresh version (*asiago pressato*)—which is the variety usually found in the United States—is smooth, soft, and tangy. It's a nice change from mozzarella or other medium-soft non-aged cheeses. If you can find the dry-aged versions, they make a nice substitute for hard aged cheeses like Parmigiano-Reggiano or pecorino Romano (see page 15).

Blue cheeses: We've had great results with imports like Gorgonzola, English Stilton, Danish Saga Blue, and French Roquefort, but there are also wonderful domestic options as well. Blue cheese has a sharp and muscular flavor that works nicely with toppings that mellow it—one classic choice is a sweet fruit like apple or pear (see page 149).

Emmenthaler, Gruyère, and standard Swiss-style cheeses: Large-holed Swiss and Swiss-style cheeses are based on cheese styles found in the Alps, which extend through Switzerland, France, Italy, Germany, and Austria. They aren't as sharp and distinctive as blue cheeses, but are definitely more assertive in flavor than mozzarella and other medium-soft cheeses. The imports (Emmenthaler from German-speaking Switzerland, and Gruyère from French-speaking Switzerland and the French Alps) are more richly flavored and meatier than typical supermarket "Swiss," but in baked pizzas the supermarket Swiss performs well (pages 160, 168, and 236). **Jarlsberg** cheese from Norway can be substituted here. Though it's not technically a Swiss cheese, the flavor, appearance, melting, and browning characteristics are very similar.

Fontina: There are Italian and Danish variations, and both are delicious—so are domestically produced versions. Fontina has a slightly sour and beefy flavor that really perks up pizzas with mild toppings (pages 69 and 121).

Soft ripened cheeses: Ripened cheeses pair beautifully with sweet fruits like apple or pear on flatbreads. Brie and Camembert are the classic French choices, and the Italian *Rosso di Langa* creates a similar effect (page 154).

Provolone: You can use this readily available Italian mild cheese wherever medium-soft cheese is called for.

Gouda and smoked gouda: Gouda, especially its aged or smoked version, has one of the "meatiest" flavors of any medium-soft cheese. It works beautifully in pizzas that showcase meats like chicken (page 124).

MEDIUM-FIRM CHEESES

Firmer cheeses get that way because of aging, which dries the cheese, firms it up, and concentrates its flavor. Grate them coarsely; they don't melt and flow well enough to be cut into large chunks like the medium-soft cheeses. An exception to this rule is *Piave*, an Italian cheese that works nicely grated or chunked.

Piave: The rich and mellow flavor of *Piave* is more assertive than mozzarella, but much less so than hard cheeses like Parmigiano-Reggiano or pecorino Romano (see page 15).

Manchego: This flavorful Spanish sheep's milk cheese makes a savory counterpoint to roasted vegetables and aromatics.

Aged cheddar: Fine aged cheddar is sublime with tomato and Italian flavors in pizza. Most of us grew up loving commercial cheddar, but the aged stuff is a completely different food, with some of the powerful flavor we taste in dry cheeses like Parmigiano. There are fantastic American and British aged cheddars, but there's even a phenomenal cheese in this style from Piedmont in Italy, called *Bra Duro*. Non-aged cheddar can be used for a more subtle but delicious pizza.

Ubriaco **and other wine-cheeses:** *Ubriaco* means drunken in Italian, and this aged cow's milk masterpiece is briefly bathed in red wine before aging, which explains its reddish rind and grapey sweetness. People have described fruity flavors in this cheese, including hints of pineapple, strawberry, and red plums. Other wine-cheeses can be substituted.

> ◌
>
> **"DOMESTIC ARTISAN CHEESES** rival the best imports—that becomes delightfully clear when traveling through (where else), Wisconsin. A specialty cheese merchant offered me a long-aged and very firm local cheddar, with an intense flavor and rich orange-brown color that did not derive from colorings. Next day, I was pleased to tell the guy how good the cheese tasted on a basic tomato and basil pizza. He was a bit appalled, because his cheese could have been served as a separate course in a meal. Maybe he's right, but I can't resist a world-class pizza topping."—Jeff

SOFT CHEESES

Apply these to pizza by dabbing or crumbling them onto the dough—use your fingers to distribute them over the surface. These cheeses are too soft to grate or cut into cubes.

Goat cheeses (soft *chèvre*): Soft goat cheese is tangy and earthy compared to cow's milk cheeses. What can we say, except that it tastes "goaty" (we mean this in the most complimentary way). Don't expect much browning.

Ricotta: Because this is a fresh, non-aged cheese, Italian imports generally aren't available. Ricotta offers a velvety texture and mellow, rich flavor. The whole-milk version tastes richer and doesn't give off as much water as the part-skim variety, but either works well in our recipes. Like soft goat cheese, ricotta doesn't brown significantly.

HARD AGED OR DRY CHEESES

These cheeses need to be coarsely grated before putting them on pizza—they don't melt and spread the way softer cheeses do.

Parmigiano-Reggiano: Parmigiano-Reggiano *(parm-ih-jano rej-ee-áno)* is a dry Italian cheese intended for grating. Its sharpness cuts through the sweet dairy flavors of softer cheeses, so Parmigiano is great when used in combination. We like to grate our own for the freshest and most powerful flavor. If you taste a chunk of delicious aged Parmigiano before grating, it may have a crunchy sensation due to crystallization of a dairy amino acid called tyrosine—this isn't a problem and is actually a sign of full aging. Less-expensive alternatives to imported Parmigiano are available everywhere, so try the domestic versions and use whichever ones you like, including pre-grated offerings.

Be aware that dry-aged cheeses like Parmigiano brown quickly in a hot oven. If you find that your dry-aged cheese is scorching, add it later in the baking cycle. It can also be grated over the top of the pizza after baking if you don't want any extra browning.

Pecorino Romano: Similar in firmness and texture to Parmigiano-Reggiano, pecorino owes its stronger flavor to its pedigree—unlike Parmigiano, it's made

Visit PizzaIn5.com, where you'll find recipes, photos, videos, and instructional material. See page 53 for outdoor grill instructions.

from sheep's milk, not cow's milk. It's also saltier, and the combination can amplify pizza flavors (or overpower them if you use too much).

Meat, Fish, Seafood, and Eggs

One of the reasons that rich Italian-style meats are so delicious on pizza is their fat, which tastes great and also carries aromatic flavors from your other ingredients to your tongue. But many sausages and pepperoni are so fatty that they can make pizza crust soggy as the fat renders. Use your judgment—if it's liberally flecked with pork fat, it's probably about 25 percent fat by weight. You can render some of the fat by briefly heating in a dry skillet or the microwave, then draining on paper towels. You generally won't need to drizzle any additional oil onto pizzas made with these kinds of meats.

Prosciutto di Parma: Prosciutto *(pro-shóot-o)* is a sweet-flavored aged ham—the authentic article is imported from Italy, but there are reasonable domestic versions available as well. Spanish Serrano ham is close to prosciutto in style, and can be substituted. The meat lends an incredible combination of sweet and savory to pizza and other flatbreads. It's lower in fat than sausage, especially if you trim excess fat (more like 10 percent fat by weight rather than 25 percent as in typical fatty sausages, or 40 percent for bacon). Given that, it doesn't need to be rendered before use.

Soppressata: This is a dried, spicy, peppery Italian salami, probably the forerunner of pepperoni (which originated and is mainly consumed in the United States). The pork in *soppressata (sope-ray-sátta)* is coarsely ground, and is meaty and toothsome compared to typical supermarket sausage. Try it instead of your usual pepperoni, and prepare for a taste sensation.

Chicken: Thigh or leg meat works better on pizza than white meat, because it stays moister despite high-temperature baking. We lightly precook chicken before using—baking, grilling, broiling, or frying all work nicely, but don't overcook.

Fish and seafood: The fish most Americans are familiar with on pizza is anchovy. This is one of those ingredients that people either love or would prefer to leave in the ocean. If your family can't all agree on anchovies, there's a simple and surprising solution: put the anchovies on *after* baking and slicing the pizza. Then there's no mystery about exactly where the anchovies are hiding and who is going to eat them. Jarred or canned anchovies don't need cooking, so fish lovers, here is your opportunity. Another opportunity to use them is in our savory *coca* with sardines (Catalan flatbread, page 178)—anchovies can be substituted here.

Another seafood item that often appears on pizza is clam—we find it convenient to use clam meat packed in 6½-ounce cans, drained of liquid and put on pizzas before cooking (one can is perfect for a 12-inch pizza). Small shrimp are also delightful.

Eggs: Most American pizza eaters haven't tried this, but it's common in parts of Italy and France. Crack an egg (or several) over the pizza after you've slid it onto the stone. In a 500°F oven, it will bake to soft-boiled perfection during the pizza's baking time, but if your oven goes to 550°F, you will need to wait 2 to 4 minutes before putting on the eggs, otherwise they will be hard-cooked. Experiment with your oven to find the best timing.

Mushrooms: Standard white mushrooms are always delicious, but we also like to use specialty varieties like cremini and portobello, which can be used in any of our recipes that call for mushrooms. Thinly sliced uncooked mushrooms can be put directly onto pizza before it goes into the oven, or you can sauté them in olive oil first for a slightly different effect. And very small wild mushrooms, if you can get them, can be strewn over pizzas whole and uncooked.

Water

We both drink filtered tap water at home, so that's what we use for dough. Assuming your own tap water tastes good enough to drink, use it filtered or unfiltered; we don't detect a flavor difference.

Yeast: Adjust It to Your Taste

Some readers of our first books preferred less yeast in their dough, but it's really a matter of taste. Less yeast will work for nearly all of our recipes, but be aware that the initial rise will be slower. We've had great results using as little as one-quarter of the specified amount of yeast. If you decrease the yeast, the initial rising time will increase to 8 hours, or even longer, depending on how much you decreased the yeast. To some people's taste, a slower rise leads to better flavor.

The other way to slow down the rise is to use cool or even cold water in the initial mix. If you try this, the rising time increases dramatically. If you also decreased the yeast, the initial rise can take 24 hours or more, so you'll need more advance planning. If you're making dough with eggs and you're contemplating a long and slow rise, do only the first 2 hours at room temperature, then transfer to the refrigerator to complete the rise (and expect a long wait). According to the U.S. Department of Agriculture, raw eggs shouldn't be at room temperature for longer than two hours (see Sources, page 281).

And one important caveat: We found we liked our gluten-free doughs with a slightly higher amount of yeast, which resulted in a lighter crust.

Throughout the book, we call for 1 tablespoon of granulated yeast for four to five pounds of dough (that's a lower dose than our other books). **You can substitute one packet of granulated yeast for a tablespoon, even though, technically speaking, those amounts aren't perfectly equivalent (1 tablespoon is 3 teaspoons, a little more than the 2¼ teaspoons found in one packet).** We've found that this makes little measurable difference in the initial rise time or in the performance of the finished dough.

> ∾
>
> **MODERN YEAST** almost never fails if used before its expiration date, so you do not need to wait until the yeast "proofs" (bubbles), nor do you need to add sugar.

We tested our recipes with Red Star brand yeast. With our approach you won't be able to tell the difference between packages labeled "active dry," "instant," "granulated," or "better for bread." Fresh cake yeast works fine as well (though you will have to increase the yeast volume by 50 percent to achieve the same rising speed). The long storage time of our doughs acts as an equalizer between all of these subtly different yeast products. **One strong recommendation: If you make dough frequently, buy yeast in bulk or in 4-ounce jars, rather than in envelopes (which are much less economical).** Food co-ops often sell yeast by the pound, in bulk (usually the Red Star brand). Make sure that bulk-purchased yeast is fresh by chatting with your co-op manager. Freeze yeast after opening to extend its shelf life, and use yeast straight from the freezer, or store smaller containers in the refrigerator (use within a few months). Between the two of us, we've had only one yeast failure in many years of baking, and it was with an outdated envelope. **The real key to avoiding yeast failures is to use water that is no warmer than lukewarm (about 100°F). Hot water kills yeast.**

After several days of high-moisture storage, yeasted dough begins to take on a flavor and aroma that approximates the flavor of natural sourdough starters

Visit PizzaIn5.com, where you'll find recipes, photos, videos, and instructional material. See page 53 for outdoor grill instructions.

used in many artisan breads. This will deepen the flavor and character of your pizzas and flatbreads.

Salt: Adjust It to Your Taste

Pizza and flatbread dough benefits from salt, which makes the dough flavorful enough to balance distinctive flavors in the toppings. Salt can also be used in a final sprinkling over pizza—if your recipe doesn't include a salty topping like olives, cured meat, or anchovies, you may prefer it with a little added salt. Plain tomato and cheese, especially if there's a second vegetable like mushrooms, can be bland without it.

All of our recipes were tested with the non-iodized, coarse Morton-brand kosher salt, measured by volume rather than weight. If you're using something finer or coarser, you need to adjust the amount. The following measurements are equivalent:

SALT-REDUCED DIET TIPS: If your doctor has recommended a low-salt diet, you can decrease the salt in these recipes as low as you'd like, even taking it out entirely (the flavor will change, of course).

- **Table salt (fine):** $^2/_3$ tablespoon
- **Morton Kosher Salt (coarse):** 1 tablespoon
- **Diamond Kosher Salt (coarsest):** $1^1/_3$ tablespoons

You can substitute sea salt, but be sure to adjust for its grind. If it's finely ground, you need to measure it like table salt above, and if it's more coarsely ground than Morton, you'll need to increase the volume accordingly. And save the really expensive artisan sea salts for sprinkling on finished products—artisan salt loses its unique flavors when baked.

Oils and Solid Fats

Olive oil: Traditional Neapolitan pizza is finished with a drizzle of olive oil before it goes into the oven. Extra-virgin varieties have the best flavor, but whatever variety you use, be careful not to overdo it, or the crust may be soft and soggy. The easiest way to get a fine drizzle is with a plastic squirt bottle.

We also use olive oil in dough to add flavor, and to tenderize, especially for dough made with higher-protein flour.

Butter: Our enriched dough recipes call for unsalted butter—if you use salted butter, you'll need to decrease salt added into the recipe. Assume 1 stick (a quarter pound or half cup) adds one-quarter teaspoon of salt to your batch and correct accordingly.

Ghee: Ghee is butter that has been clarified and slightly toasted. It is a staple in Indian kitchens because of its wonderful flavor. Since the heat-sensitive milk solids are toasted and then strained off, ghee can be heated to a much higher temperature than regular butter. It can be found in many Asian markets, but we often make our own. The following recipe makes three-quarters of a pound (about 1$\frac{2}{3}$ cups).

1. Melt 1 pound of unsalted butter in a medium saucepan over low heat. When it is completely melted, bring it up to a boil and continue until it is frothy.

Visit PizzaIn5.com, where you'll find recipes, photos, videos, and instructional material. See page 53 for outdoor grill instructions.

2. Reduce the heat to low and cook gently until the milk solids have settled on the bottom of the pot and are golden brown.

3. Strain the ghee through a fine-mesh sieve. Allow it to cool completely, cover, and refrigerate. The ghee will last in the refrigerator for 1 month.

Sweeteners

Sweeteners are frequently used in pizza dough, especially in the United States. Why did sweeteners become common here? One reason is that hard-wheat flours—those high in protein and usually labeled as "bread flour"—grow particularly well in North America. But high-protein flours can make tough pizzas, especially when baked at high temperature and when whole grain is included. Sweetener, when used in small doses, acts as a tenderizer, especially with a little oil. You can use plain sugar, or any of the natural sweeteners we list. In the amounts we use in pizza, you can use them interchangeably; the differences in water content aren't important. Sweeteners are used more generously to add flavor in American-style pizza dough (page 78) and in enriched doughs (pages 251–260). For these sweeter doughs, we don't recommend interchanging honey, sugar, and agave; flavor and performance differences will matter for these amounts.

Sugar: Plain granulated white sugar, from either cane or sugar beets, works equally well as a tenderizer or sweetener in our recipes.

Honey: Many readers of our second book, ***Healthy Bread in Five Minutes a Day,*** preferred honey and other natural sweeteners. Like other sweeteners, honey works well as a tenderizer in pizza, and adds terrific flavor to sweet flatbreads.

Malt powder: Malt powder is available in either "diastatic" or "non-diastatic" varieties. Diastatic malt has enzymes that help yeast to use sugars and become active quickly, whereas non-diastatic is strictly a sweetener rich in barley malt sugar (maltose). We've found that diastatic malt's active enzymes just aren't important for long-stored doughs—the yeast doesn't need to be in a hurry. Plus, diastatic malt can make doughs looser than they should be. So use non-diastatic malt powder when you use malt as a tenderizer or for flavor in pizza or flatbread dough.

Agave syrup: Agave syrup (sometimes labeled "agave nectar") tastes the tiniest bit like tequila, and no wonder. The agave plant is the source of the fermentable juice that makes the world's best tequila, and agave syrup is the concentrated sweetener made from that juice.

Visit PizzaIn5.com, where you'll find recipes, photos, videos, and instructional material. See page 53 for outdoor grill instructions.

3

EQUIPMENT

Most of the same fun toys used for baking bread can be reused to make great pizza and flatbread. You don't need to spend an arm and a leg, but there are a few items that will make the job easier and help you create the perfect pizza crust. The four most useful items are:

1. Baking stone, cast-iron pizza pan, or perforated pizza pan

2. Pizza peel

3. Oven thermometer

4. Dough scraper

The others are nice, but not absolutely necessary. See Sources (page 281) to locate mail-order and Web-based vendors for harder-to-find items.

Equipment for Baking Pizzas and Flatbreads

Baking stone, cast-iron pizza pan, or cast-iron skillet: In *Artisan Bread in Five Minutes a Day*, and in *Healthy Bread in Five Minutes a Day*, our testing showed that crusts come out browner, crispier, and tastier when the dough is baked on a ceramic or masonry baking stone. They may be labeled "pizza stones" (usually round), or "baking stones" (usually rectangular), but they're both made from the same kinds of materials and perform the same way. To get the pizza onto the hot stone, you slide it off of a pizza peel (see page 27). If you think crust is important to loaf breads, you better believe it's important to pizza and flatbread, where so much of the experience is the crust. Look for 1/2-inch-thick stones because thinner ones are more likely to crack with frequent use. In our experience, stones don't last forever—but the thick ones are pretty durable. They do take longer to preheat compared to thinner ones, or cast iron (see below).

Traditionally, bakers have given two reasons for the success of dough that bakes right on a stone, whether flatbread, pizza, or loaf bread. First, the stone promotes fast, even, and powerful heat transfer because of its weight and density, resulting in a crisp crust. That intense heat transfer also promotes terrific "oven spring," especially in home ovens that don't necessarily provide perfectly even heat. "Oven spring" is the sudden expansion of gases within the flatbread that occurs upon contact with the hot oven air and the hot surface it rests on. That prevents a dense, tough result. Second, it's always been assumed that the stone's porosity allows it to absorb excess moisture from dough (especially wet dough), encouraging crispness.

It turns out that it must be mostly explanation number one, because we've found that bread and pizza baked on preheated cast-iron pizza pans, and even in preheated cast-iron skillets, are just as crisp as those baked on stones, de-spite the fact that cast iron isn't porous at all (see Chapter 4, Tips and Tech-niques for Perfect Pizza and Flatbread, page 49, for more about using cast iron).

Having said all this, you can make decent pizza without a baking stone; just do it right on a baking sheet (see "Heavy-Gauge Baking Sheets," page 31). The crust won't be as crisp, but the result will be better than most any pizza you can buy.

Pizza peel: This is a flat board with a long handle used to slide bread or pizza onto a hot stone. You can't use anything made of plastic to transfer pizza or flatbread into the oven—it could melt upon contact with the hot baking stone. Cover the peel with flour, cornmeal, or parchment paper before putting dough on it or everything will stick to the peel (and possibly to the stone). If you don't have a pizza peel, a flat cookie sheet with no sides will do, but it will be more difficult to handle. Another alternative is a wood cutting board shaped with a handle.

Other Equipment

Oven thermometer: Home ovens are often off by 50 to 75 degrees, and this can make it very difficult to achieve successful pizza or flatbread crust, so it's important to use an oven thermometer. A simple inexpensive one should run less than $20.00. If your oven runs on the hot side, this is going to be trouble-some for sweet crusts, which can scorch in a too-hot oven (reducing the baking time may help). One caveat—if your oven runs hot and you know it, you might appreciate quick-baked pizza done in a very hot oven—the ovens in Naples achieve 905°F (see page 39). Jeff's home oven reaches 600°F at its 550°F set-ting, and he's not getting it recalibrated! If you're baking sweet flatbreads in

Visit PizzaIn5.com, where you'll find recipes, photos, videos, and instructional material. See page 53 for outdoor grill instructions.

an oven that runs hot, adjust the temperature downward based on the oven thermometer's reading. But pizzas intended to have a crisp crust won't do well if your oven's running cool—you end up with a soft crust and a long baking time. So if your oven's running cool, you may want to get it recalibrated by a professional.

Be aware that an oven thermometer may take longer to reflect the final temperature than the 30-minute preheat we specify.

Dough scraper: A metal dough scraper (also called a bench scraper) makes it much easier to make flatbread and pizza crust using wet dough. Without one, there'll be the temptation to use too much flour to prevent dough from sticking to the work surface. As you stretch your dough, dust it with flour and scrape it off the work surface if it sticks—don't work the flour into the dough. The scraper is also the easiest way to scrape excess flour, cornmeal, or crumbs off a hot baking stone between pizzas.

Here are more items that we use to make the process easier, in the order they are used in the process:

A bucket, large plastic storage container, or a glass, stainless steel, or crockery container with a lid: You can use a 5- or 6-quart bowl (ceramic, glass, or stainless steel) covered with plastic wrap to mix and store dough. Don't cover it with a towel, which sticks to our wet dough. Or, use a stainless steel cooking pot with a lid.

Many people find a covered bucket is much more convenient. Feel free to mix and store the dough in the same vessel—this will save you from washing one more item (it all figures into the five minutes a day). Look for a food-grade container that holds about five quarts, to allow for the initial rise. Round containers are a little easier to mix in than square ones, which catch flour in the corners. Some food storage buckets include a vent for microwave steaming, which can be opened to let carbon dioxide and alcohol vapor escape during the fermentation process. Another vented option is a beer-making bucket, which is sold at home-brewing stores. You can close the vent (or seal the lid) after the first two days because gas production has slowed by then. If your bread has an alcohol smell, you need more venting, or need to leave the vent open longer (not everyone can detect this alcohol buildup as most of it boils off during baking and subsequent evaporation). If you don't have a vented container, just leave the lid open a crack for the first few days of storage, or drill a very small hole in a plastic lid.

Don't use screw-top containers, unless you're very careful about leaving them open a crack—their airtight seal could theoretically trap fermentation gases under pressure and shatter the container. Never completely tighten a screw-top, even late in the batch's life.

Measuring cups: Avoid 2-cup measuring cups, because they overestimate flour quantity when using the scoop-and-sweep method (see sidebar, page 62), due to excessive packing-down into the cup. And be sure to use *dry* measuring cups for flour, which reflect the labeled volume when leveled to the top. Liquid measuring cups are great for water and oil, but you can't level off a liquid measuring cup filled with flour.

Measuring spoons: Seek out a set that includes a half-tablespoon measure— some of our recipes call for 1½ tablespoons. If you can't find a half-tablespoon measure, you can approximate it by using a rounded teaspoon, or, to be more exact, measure out 1½ teaspoons.

Scale: We have come to prefer weighing ingredients, rather than using measuring cups. Luckily, digital scales are getting cheaper all the time. Chapter 4, Tips and Techniques, contains tables of weight and volume equivalents (including metric units) on pages 36–38, and you can use them to convert recipes from volumes to weights. Just press "tare" or "zero" after each ingredient is added to the dough vessel and you can use these scales without slowing down to do the arithmetic.

The scale is also a nice, consistent way to measure out a half-pound piece of dough for pizza, but it isn't absolutely necessary, because we also give you a visual cue for dough weight (for example, an orange-size piece is about one-half pound of dough—see the chart in Chapter 4, Tips and Techniques, page 41.)

Dough whisk: Danish-style dough whisks are made from strong non-bendable wire on a wood handle, and they're used to blend liquid and dry ingredients together quickly in the dough bucket. We find that they work faster and offer less resistance than a traditional wooden spoon—though a wooden spoon works fine.

Food processors and mixers: You can use a 14-cup food processor (with dough attachment) or a heavy-duty stand mixer (with paddle) rather than a spoon or dough whisk to mix the dough.

Immersion blenders: These are great for blending a chunk of old dough with water. The resulting mixture can be used to jump-start the development of sourdough flavor in your new batch of stored dough (see sidebar, page 68). These blenders are also nice for breaking up tomato for pizza sauce. Be sure that the immersion blender is fully submerged in the liquid mixture before turning it on, otherwise you'll be spattered with ingredients. **Safety note:** Remember that immersion blenders don't have protective safety interlocks, so it's possible to touch the sharp spinning blades while the unit is running. Be careful, and don't let children use these.

Kitchen shears/scissors: It's a snap to use a scissors for cutting pita bread or pizza into wedges—much easier than a knife. They're also great for cutting pieces of dough out of your storage vessel (or just use a serrated knife), and for snipping fresh herbs.

Rolling pin: Skinny French rolling pins that look like a large dowel, both tapered and straight, work just as well as the pins with handles. We have tried them all and have determined that wood, marble, and metal all get the job done; we've even rolled out the dough with a bottle of wine in a pinch. Just use what is most comfortable for you.

Nonslip rubber mat: One way to minimize cleanup is to roll your pizza dough right on a pizza peel rather than on the counter or a board. If you use a rolling pin rather than hand-stretching, the pizza peel will tend to move while you roll. Using a simple non-slip rubber mat under the pizza peel prevents this movement and really makes it easier to get the job done. Look for a perforated version that is dishwasher-safe.

In a pinch, you can use a kitchen towel or damp paper towel the same way.

Heavy-gauge baking sheets, jelly-roll pans, and cookie sheets: The highest-quality baking sheets are made of super-heavyweight aluminum and have short rims (sometimes called a jelly-roll pan). When well greased with olive oil, they are a good alternative to the pizza peel/baking stone method for pizza baking. In addition to letting you avoid the slide off the pizza peel onto a stone, baking sheets are also nice for more heavily topped pizzas—the short rim keeps things in place if something melts off the top.

Visit PizzaIn5.com, where you'll find recipes, photos, videos, and instructional material. See page 53 for outdoor grill instructions.

Similar-gauge flat round pans are available specifically for pizza. Avoid "air-insulated" baking sheets—they don't conduct heat well and won't produce a crisp crust. Thin cookie sheets can be used, but like air-insulated bakeware, they won't produce a great crust.

Parchment paper: Parchment paper is an alternative to flour or cornmeal for preventing pizza from sticking to the pizza peel as it's slid into the oven. Use a paper that's temperature-rated to withstand what's called for in the recipe you're using. The paper goes with the pizza onto the preheated stone, and can be removed halfway through baking to crisp up the bottom crust (see page 48). Don't use products labeled "pastry parchment," which stick miserably to baked dough. Parchment paper is also used for separating dough disks for freezing (see page 51). Never try to substitute wax paper for parchment—it will melt.

Silicone mats: Nonstick, flexible silicone baking mats are convenient and are reusable thousands of times. They're terrific for lower-temperature recipes (like sweet flatbreads), but we find that pizzas and other lean-dough specialties don't crisp very well on silicone. They're used on top of a cookie sheet or dropped onto a hot stone, and don't need to be greased, so cleanup is a breeze. Be sure to get a mat rated to the temperature you need—they're generally not rated for high-temperature baking.

Perforated pizza pans and screen-style pizza pans: Perforated pizza pans come close to creating the crust you get with stones and cast iron, but they achieve it a different way—by allowing hot oven air to reach the underside of the pizza. Pizza pans made from a screen-like material work the same way.

Pie tins: Ten-inch pie tins are great for focaccia (page 183) because they produce a more uniform shape and keep oil and toppings from leaking into your oven. We use metal pans, but glass or ceramic also do a great job. If your pie tins are smaller your focaccia will tend to be thicker, unless you reduce the amount of dough slightly.

Deep-dish pizza pans: In Chicago they use a special round pan for making the traditional deep-dish pizza, which is about 12 to 14 inches wide and 1½ to 2 inches deep. These pans are wonderful, but a bit too large for home use. We've also had good results with a 2-inch-deep cake pan. For individual Chicago deep-dish pizzas we found a small 6×1-inch cast-iron dish made by Lodge (see the color insert). For the *torta* (page 193) we prefer to use a shallow springform pan, which doesn't require lifting out the pizza.

Pastry brush: These are used to paint egg wash, oil, or water onto the surface of flatbreads just before baking. We both prefer the bristle ones to the silicone—we find them easier to control—but that's a matter of taste.

Squirt bottle: A squirt bottle is a great way to store and dispense olive oil; it prevents you from applying too much. You can also get a removable pourer that fits the top of your olive oil bottle, which serves the same purpose and is reusable.

Mandoline: In several recipes we call for ingredients to be sliced very thin. You can achieve this with a sharp knife and a steady hand, but the easiest way is to slice on a mandoline. It looks like a miniature guillotine and is incredibly sharp, so be very careful when using one, and use the guard that comes with it. There are very expensive metal versions, but we have found the inexpensive plastic ones work just as well and they tend to be less fussy and easier to clean.

Ovens: Most home ovens have a maximum temperature setting of either 500°F or 550°F. Use an oven thermometer to determine whether your oven is actually achieving this temperature (this may take longer than the 30-minute

Visit PizzaIn5.com, where you'll find recipes, photos, videos, and instructional material. See page 53 for outdoor grill instructions.

preheat we specify in our recipes). For most pizzas made with lean dough, the hotter the better. If your oven's top setting is 500°F (not 550°F), your bake time will be about 15 percent longer than what we call for in the recipes.

Convection ovens: By circulating hot air with a powerful fan, convection ovens transfer heat more quickly, so baking time can be reduced by 15 percent and oven heat needs to be decreased by 25 degrees. Convection promotes browning of the top crust and the toppings. **Watch carefully for overbrowning or burning of toppings if you select the convection mode—in some ovens, you can burn the top before the bottom is crisp.** It may be helpful to turn the pizza or flatbread around at the halfway point, so that each side is exposed directly to the fan. Ignore any convection oven instructions that claim you can skip the preheat—that will produce a soft crust. As always, use an oven thermometer to check oven temperature; air circulation can fool thermostats in some models. These instructions apply only to range-based convection ovens, not microwaves with convection modes, which we have not tested.

Wood-fired oven: It certainly would be nice to have a brick or masonry wood-fired outdoor oven, puffing away in the backyard at 900°F. We'd flash-bake the crust to a perfect crunch in 90 seconds. But it's not just the crust that excels in a hot wood-fired oven—that quick bake gives you toppings that retain their shape and freshness. And the wood fire imparts a subtle, smoky flavor. But alas, neither of us owns a wood-fired oven (yet). A terrific book on building your own is *The Bread Builders: Hearth Loaves and Masonry Ovens* by Daniel Wing and Alan Scott.

Cooling rack: These are fashioned out of wire or thin metal and are very helpful in preventing the soggy bottom crust that can result when you cool pizza on a plate or other nonporous surface.

4

TIPS AND TECHNIQUES FOR PERFECT PIZZA AND FLATBREAD MADE WITH STORED DOUGH

This chapter will help you perfect your pizzas and flatbreads made from our stored high-moisture doughs. With just a little effort, you can produce results as professional and impressive as the best pizzerias.

Measuring Ingredients by Weight

Weight equivalents can be a terrific advantage if you do a lot of baking—using them is just quicker than using measuring cups. With digital scales, it's a snap—just press the "tare" (zeroing) button before adding an ingredient to the mixing vessel, then press "tare" again to add the next ingredient. The scale does all the arithmetic for you. Following are some useful U.S. and metric equivalents so you can convert any recipe in the book to a weighed version (the master dough recipes are already done). Be aware that the tables reflect minor rounding errors, which shouldn't affect your recipes. **All cup measurements were calculated using the scoop-and-sweep method described in Chapter 5, page 62.**

INGREDIENT	VOLUME (U.S.)	WEIGHT (U.S. OUNCES)	WEIGHT (GRAMS)
Unbleached all-purpose flour	1 cup	5	140
Bleached all-purpose flour	1 cup	5	140
Bread flour (high-protein flour)	1 cup	5	140
Whole wheat flour (traditional or white)	1 cup	4½	130
King Arthur Flour Italian-Style Flour ("00" type)	1 cup	4½	130
Durum flour (semolina)	1 cup	6	170
Brown rice flour	1 cup	5½	160
Cake flour, bleached	1 cup	4	115
Cornstarch	1 cup	4½	130
Rye flour, whole grain	1 cup	4¼	120
Sorghum flour	1 cup	4¾	135
Spelt flour, whole grain	1 cup	4½	130
Tapioca flour (starch)	1 cup	4½	130
Teff flour	1 cup	5¼	150
White rice flour	1 cup	5	140
King Arthur Unbleached Cake Flour	1 cup	5	140
Cornmeal (white or yellow)	1 cup	5¾	165

(continued)

INGREDIENT	VOLUME (U.S.)	WEIGHT (U.S. OUNCES)	WEIGHT (GRAMS)
Corn masa (*masa harina*)	1 cup	4	115
Cocoa powder	½ cup	2	55
Vegetable oil (canola, olive, etc)	½ cup	3¾	110
Butter, 1 stick (¼ pound)	½ cup (8 tablespoons)	4	115
Water	1 cup	8	225
Honey	½ cup	6	170
Raisins	½ cup	3	85
White granulated sugar	1 cup	7	200
Brown sugar, packed	1 cup	8	225
Malt powder, non-diastatic	2 tablespoons	1	25
Yeast, granulated	1 tablespoon	0.35	10
Salt, kosher (Morton brand)	1 tablespoon	0.63	17

Conversion Tables for Common Measures

VOLUMES		
U.S. SPOON AND CUP MEASURES	U.S. VOLUME	METRIC VOLUME
1 teaspoon	⅙ ounce	5 ml
1 tablespoon	½ ounce	15 ml
¼ cup (4 tablespoons)	2 ounces	60 ml

(continued)

Visit PizzaIn5.com, where you'll find recipes, photos, videos, and instructional material. See page 53 for outdoor grill instructions.

U.S. SPOON AND CUP MEASURES	U.S. VOLUME	METRIC VOLUME
½ cup (8 tablespoons)	4 ounces	120 ml
1 cup	8 ounces	240 ml
2 cup	16 ounces	475 ml
4 cups	32 ounces	950 ml

U.S. AND METRIC WEIGHT CONVERSIONS		
U.S. WEIGHT (OUNCES)	U.S. WEIGHT (POUNDS)	METRIC WEIGHT
1 ounce	⅟₁₆ pound	28 grams
2 ounces	⅛ pound	56 grams
4 ounces	¼ pound	112 grams
8 ounces	½ pound	225 grams
16 ounces	1 pound	455 grams

OVEN TEMPERATURE: FAHRENHEIT TO CELSIUS CONVERSION	
DEGREES FAHRENHEIT (°F)	DEGREES CELSIUS (°C)
350	180
375	190
400	200
425	220
450	230
475	240
500	250
550	288

Weighing Small-Quantity Ingredients

Our recipes only require a fraction of an ounce for some ingredients (like salt and yeast). Since many scales for home use are accurate only to within the nearest eighth of an ounce (3 or 4 grams), measuring small amounts this way can introduce inaccuracy, but this becomes less important when measuring larger quantities for doubled recipes. Experiment with scales; some are better than others for weighing small amounts of ingredients. If you find one that gives consistent results for yeast and salt in typical quantities, by all means use it.

Frequently Asked Questions from Readers

"CAN YOU MAKE AUTHENTIC NEAPOLITAN PIZZA IN YOUR HOME KITCHEN?"

The Italians call it *verace pizza Napoletana (ver-á-chay pizza nap-o-lih-tána)*—authentic Naples-style pizza. But can you re-create it at home? Probably not, at least not as the Italian government defines it. The authorities have declared thin-crusted, crisp-but-tender Neapolitan pizza as a national treasure worthy of protection (it is). Your home kitchen almost certainly won't meet the requirements, but if you can achieve a thin crust, your result will be utterly delicious anyway (see Chapter 5).

A few items from the government list of absolute requirements for *verace pizza Napoletana*:

- *pizza Margherita*, the classic Neapolitan pie, is made only with tomato, basil, and mozzarella cheese.
- The pizza must be baked in a wood-fired oven (not coal, gas, or electric) at 905°F.

Visit PizzaIn5.com, where you'll find recipes, photos, videos, and instructional material. See page 53 for outdoor grill instructions.

- The flour must be Italian type "00" (fine-ground, low-protein) with the addition of a small amount of "0" (a little higher in protein, see page 5).
- The dough *may not* contain olive oil. But you *must* drizzle olive oil on top, just before putting it into the oven.
- Restaurant owners may not allow patrons to remove the pizza from the *pizzeria* to be eaten elsewhere or later. If they do, the pizza may not be called *"pizza Napoletana"* (we're not making this up). So much for breakfast leftovers.
- You may not use a rolling pin. Ever. Just your hands and fingers. It takes a fair amount of practice to get a thin crust without a rolling pin, especially with wet doughs like ours. But it's really fun, and if you're interested, see the hand-stretching dough section, pages 42–44.

"HOW MUCH TOPPING SHOULD I USE ON PIZZA?"

In general, thin-crusted pizzas, with dough stretched to $\frac{1}{8}$ inch thick or less, come out better if you use less topping. Lightly topped pizzas develop crisper crusts and are easier to slide off the pizza peel. We generally specify about 3 ounces of cheese, and 3 ounces of sauce, even though typical American pizzas have more than that—they tend to have thicker crusts. If you want a cheesier, saucier pizza, consider using more dough, and stretch it to a thickness of one-quarter inch or more.

"HOW THICK SHOULD THE CRUST BE?"

Here's how we do it:

You'll notice that most of our recipes assume Neapolitan (Naples style) thickness (one-eighth inch). If you want to change the thickness, just vary the dough quantity as we suggest in the following chart.

PIZZA STYLE	DOUGH THICKNESS	DOUGH NEEDED
Superthin style; cracker crust	1/16 inch	1/4 pound (peach-size) for 12-inch round
Pizzette	1/8 inch	2 ounces (golf ball-size) for 4-inch round
Neapolitan (Naples style)	1/8 inch	1/2 pound (orange-size) for 12-inch round
American style, or Roman thick-style	1/4 inch	1 pound (grapefruit-size) for 12-inch round
Sicilian style; extra thick	1/2 inch	2 pounds (small-cantaloupe size) for 18 × 13-inch baking sheet
Focaccia (see below)	3/4 inch	3/4 pound (large-orange size) for 10-inch pie tin

"WHAT'S THE DIFFERENCE BETWEEN PIZZA AND FOCACCIA?"

Some will argue, but we prefer to just eat and enjoy. The short answer is that pizza is thin-crusted, and focaccia is thicker. Pizza dough is rolled or stretched to about one-eighth-inch thickness before baking, while focaccia is about three-quarter inch thick before baking. In addition, the toppings tend to be different. Focaccia is not topped with cheese and tomato, rather, it tends to features vegetables and herbs, and is rich in olive oil. There are endless variations, but the classic is a simple topping of sautéed onion and rosemary. You can convert many of the recipes in this book to focaccia by forming a thicker round of dough, modifying the toppings, and using plenty of good-quality olive oil.

Visit PizzaIn5.com, where you'll find recipes, photos, videos, and instructional material. See page 53 for outdoor grill instructions.

"HOW DO YOU MAKE VERY THIN-CRUSTED PIZZA (CRACKER CRUST)?"

Making really thin crust that doesn't tear takes a bit of practice, and we can't do it without a rolling pin. You need to get to one-sixteenth of an inch, and this will take a bit of time. Once you're ready for toppings, remember that you need to use less—a crust this thin just can't support much weight and moisture without becoming soggy, and the goal here is a crisp pizza. If you use less sauce, cheese, vegetables, and meat you can succeed with this somewhat temperamental method. Bake at the usual temperature but check earlier to prevent scorching.

To achieve crispness in a cracker crust, you may need to bake the crust "blind" before adding toppings (see page 48). This will take a bit of trial and error, depending on your oven.

"SHOULD DOUGH FOR PIZZA AND FLATBREADS BE HAND-STRETCHED?"

Some pizza connoisseurs insist that great pizza crust can't be made using a rolling pin, but we're not so sure. When we teach classes, we usually roll out pizza dough on a floured surface with a pin, and the results are wonderful. But this is a matter of taste, so we're going to describe how hand-stretched pizza

(or flatbread) is done. These techniques are helpful even if you do use a rolling pin to help get it thin—the pin doesn't completely replace hand-stretching. Who knows, you may someday find yourself without a pin and you may need to stretch a pizza by hand. Preferably on a desert island equipped with a wood-fired oven . . .

1. Dust the surface of the refrigerated dough with flour and cut off a ½-pound (orange-size) piece. Dust with more flour and quickly shape it into a ball by stretching the surface of the dough around to the bottom on all four sides, rotating the ball a quarter-turn as you go.

2. Allow the ball to sit for 20 to 40 minutes under a sheet of plastic wrap or covered with an overturned roomy bowl. This allows the gluten to relax, and that will help you stretch the dough more easily. In fact, if you have time, this makes the rolling-pin method easier, too. If you don't have time, you can omit this step, but you'll be wrestling with the dough a little more.

3. Dust with flour (use lots, and don't be shy about sprinkling on more), then flatten and stretch the ball on a floured work surface, pressing straight down with your fingertips to spread and enlarge the disk. Lift and hang the dough so gravity can do some of the work for you (we like draping it over our forearms). When it begins to flatten, place it on top of the backs of your hands. Gently turn and spin the disk with your knuckles so as to stretch it without tearing. Concentrate on stretching the edge, not the center; this will help prevent holes from forming.

Visit PizzaIn5.com, where you'll find recipes, photos, videos, and instructional material. See page 53 for outdoor grill instructions.

4. Optional: Throw the dough up in the air (see sidebar, Chapter 5, page 65, for instructions).

5. Continue in this fashion until the disk is about ⅛ inch thick. The edge will be slightly thicker.

"WHAT IS THE KEY TO SUCCESS IN SLIDING A PIZZA OFF A PEEL? PREPARE AND MEASURE OUT ALL TOPPINGS IN ADVANCE."

When you're trying to slide a pizza off of a peel and onto a hot stone, you don't want it to stick. Otherwise you'll have a big mess in your oven when the toppings shoot off your pizza. **Timing is key here,** because the longer the dough sits on the pizza peel, the more likely it is to stick. Prepare and measure all your toppings in advance, readying them in small bowls or ramekins. Dust the pizza peel with more flour before laying the dough onto it. Top quickly and top lightly—the more you use, the heavier the dough will sit on the peel. **Cornmeal instead of flour on the pizza peel?** It's really a matter of taste. If you cover the pizza peel with cornmeal rather than flour, you'll get a crunchy, corny, toasty bottom crust (see sidebar, page 45). It can cause more smoking in the oven, though, so use your exhaust fan.

For the most reliable slide, place the tip of the peel near the back of the stone, close to where you want the far edge of the pizza to land. Give the peel

a few quick forward-and-back jiggles and pull it sharply out from under the pizza. If you still aren't confident, build your pizza on parchment paper—the parchment slides right onto the stone with the pizza and can be removed halfway through baking. Or bake directly on a greased baking sheet and you won't have to do any sliding at all.

"IS THERE TOO MUCH FLOUR (OR CORNMEAL) ON THE BOTTOM OF THE CRUST?"

As you're learning the techniques for stretching pizza dough, you'll want to err on the side of dusting with lots of flour (see "The Key to Success in Sliding a Pizza Off a Peel," page 44). But you may find that *too* much flour under the pizza interferes with the flavor and feel of the crust. The same thing can happen with cornmeal, if that's what you're using. Three pieces of advice:

IS CORNMEAL ON THE BOTTOM OF A PIZZA AUTHENTICALLY ITALIAN? Well, probably not. A few years ago, a major U.S. pizza chain restaurant redesigned its pizzas, and debated whether or not to use cornmeal on the pizza peel, or just flour. They searched as far as Italy, where they found that only flour is used there. But in taste tests, many U.S. consumers preferred the crunch and flavor of cornmeal under the pizza, so that's what they went with. We like both, but cornmeal causes more smoke problems if you use lots and it burns on the stone.

Visit PizzaIn5.com, where you'll find recipes, photos, videos, and instructional material. See page 53 for outdoor grill instructions.

1. After baking, you can scrape excess flour or cornmeal off the bottom of a pizza with a knife; just lift one side and scrape, then turn the pizza to complete the job.

2. As you get more experienced, try to use the minimum amount of flour or cornmeal necessary to prevent sticking; this should make the scraping step unnecessary.

3. Consider the parchment paper option (see page 32).

"WHY SUCH SMALL PIZZAS?"

A half-pound of dough makes a 12-inch pizza when rolled to a thickness of one-eighth inch. Start with pies this size because they're much easier to handle when you're learning the method. As you become confident that your pizza won't stick to the peel when you slide it in, you can use bigger pieces of dough and make bigger pizzas. The biggest pizzas are most easily made in large rectangular baking sheets (see page 31).

"HELP, MY PIZZA DOUGH IS STUCK TO THE PEEL!"

We always tell people to keep shaking the pizza peel while building their pies to be sure that the dough isn't sticking, and to do this before you get to the oven—you don't want any nasty surprises. If you find that it's not moving well before the toppings are put on (or any time before the oven-slide), you need to get things unstuck. Here's what you do:

1. Locate where the dough is sticking by shaking the peel and watching how the dough moves. The dough will move but not around the stuck spot.

2. Sprinkle a little flour on the peel next to the spot that is stuck. Using a dough scraper (see page 28) held at a shallow angle, push the flour under the dough, lifting it by moving toward the center as far as necessary to unstick the spot that isn't moving.

3. Shake the peel again to confirm your success. If it's still not moving, repeat.

"I'M AFRAID OF SLIDING PIZZAS OFF A PIZZA PEEL. CAN I ASSEMBLE AND BAKE PIZZA RIGHT ON A NON-PREHEATED BAKING SHEET?"

Absolutely. Though we think the crust isn't quite as crisp when done this way, it's a nice alternative for achieving delicious pizza without the need to slide your pizza off a peel. It's also a handy way to make really large pizzas, which are tricky to slide into the oven. Heavy-gauge aluminum sheets are the best, especially those with short-rimmed sides to contain any errant toppings (see page 31). They're known in the baking trade as "half sheets," or jelly-roll pans. Aluminum heats up quickly in the oven and it's that sudden heating that gives you a crisp crust. Here's what you do:

1. Generously grease a heavy-gauge baking sheet with olive oil.

2. Stretch your dough to the desired thickness and place it on the baking sheet; press and stretch further if desired.

3. Cover with toppings and place into a preheated oven right on a hot stone (if you have one) sitting on a low shelf. Baking time may increase slightly.

Visit PizzaIn5.com, where you'll find recipes, photos, videos, and instructional material. See page 53 for outdoor grill instructions.

"WHAT IS 'LEAN' DOUGH?"

"Lean" doughs (pages 59–98) are those made without significant eggs, fat, dairy, or sweetener. Lean doughs bake well without burning or drying out at high temperatures. Doughs "enriched" with lots of eggs, fat, dairy, or sweeteners require a lower baking temperature.

"HOW DO YOU PREVENT A SOGGY PIZZA CRUST, OR ONE THAT WON'T BROWN OR BECOME CRISP?"

Our dough is wetter than most, and that's what allows it to be stored. But that means you have to be careful not to pile on too many toppings. Otherwise, you'll be at risk for a soggy crust. In general, we recommend that you use toppings and sauces sparingly, and prepare them so that excess water is reduced—either squeezed away or cooked away. If you really want a drier crust, or if you like lots of toppings or a thicker crust, consider baking the crust "blind." Here's how: Dock (puncture) the crust well with the times of a fork and bake at the usual temperature, *without any toppings*, for about 5 minutes. Occasionally peek through the oven window and, if the crust is puffing like pita bread, reach in (carefully) and poke it with a fork (a long-handled barbecue fork works well). When the crust is just beginning to brown (don't overdo it), remove from the oven, add cheese and toppings, and complete the baking. **Baking "blind" is a must when baking pizza directly on the grates of a gas grill,** but isn't necessary if you use a stone on the gas grill (see page 53).

If you are baking on parchment paper or a nonstick silicone mat, these may prevent your bottom crust from crisping up as much as you like. To get the desired crust, check the bottom crust after about 8 minutes of baking; if it is not browning, slide the pizza off the parchment or silicone mat and finish baking directly on the pizza stone or oven rack to crisp it up.

In some ovens the top crust can come out a bit pale, even though it is thoroughly baked. One way to achieve a crisp wood-fired oven look is to put the baked pizza under the broiler for a couple of minutes (see Stovetop Pizza, page 170).

"WHY SUCH A SHORT PREHEAT?"

Some traditional pizza books suggest preheating a baking stone for an hour, to absorb all the heat it possibly can, but we specify a 30-minute preheat. Many of our readers express concern about the wasted energy for a long preheat, not to mention the need for more advance planning (committing to a long preheat makes getting flatbread on the table for weeknight dinners a longer endeavor). So we compromised—we know that many ovens will produce a crisper crust with a longer preheat, but we're pretty happy with the results we get at 30 minutes (even though many ovens equipped with a stone won't quite achieve maximum temperature that soon). If you have the time (especially if it's winter, when a toasty kitchen is a bonus), try preheating for 45 or even 60 minutes. It's not essential but it can be nice.

If you find that your toppings are overbrowning before the crust is crisp, that can be a sign that you might need the longer preheat; be aware that your baking time may decrease by 15 to 25 percent, though you may get some improvement just by lowering the shelf with your stone to the bottom of the oven. If you really want to go to a short preheat, consider switching to a cast-iron pizza pan, which heats up faster than ceramic baking stones (see page 26).

"HOW BROWN SHOULD PIZZA CHEESE GET?"

Like so many things in the world of pizza, this is a matter of taste. Classic Neapolitan pizza is baked so hot (905°F), and therefore so fast, that there's little time for the cheese to brown (caramelize). In home ovens, the highest oven setting doesn't get past 550°F, and in some, just 500°F. This means that there's more time for cheese to caramelize, which can deepen its flavor (be careful not

Visit PizzaIn5.com, where you'll find recipes, photos, videos, and instructional material. See page 53 for outdoor grill instructions.

to let it burn). We found that the bottom-most shelf in most home ovens was the best place for your pizza stone or iron. It allows the crust to crisp before the cheese overcaramelizes and burns.

But as always, every oven is different, so experiment and do it the way you love best. Try different shelf positions if you're not getting the results you want.

"HOW DO YOU PROTECT TOPPINGS FROM SCORCHING AND BURNING?"

We bake our pizzas in hot ovens for wonderful crisp crusts and flash-baked toppings that don't reduce down to soup with long cooking. The problem with such a hot oven is that some toppings, especially vegetables, can burn (eggplant is a typical suspect). If a topping ingredient is burning before the rest of the pizza is finished, there's an easy solution: protect it with cheese. Just change the order for applying the toppings. Although it's often picturesque to start with cheese and finish with other toppings, switch it around to finish with cheese, and you'll protect more easily scorched vegetable ingredients.

"WHY DO YOU CUT MEDIUM-SOFT CHEESE INTO CHUNKS RATHER THAN GRATING OR SLICING IT?"

We found that sliced or grated mozzarella cheese sometimes overbrowned, or even burned, before the crust was nicely baked and crisp—this was true of all the medium-soft cheeses (see page 10). When we tried half-inch *chunks* of cheese, the extra time it took for the cheese to melt and spread gave the crust the head start it needed to crisp just at the moment that the cheese had browned the way we like it. Space out the cheese chunks well; they'll spread to fill in the spaces between the other toppings. This only applies to oven-baked pizza—**if you're baking on the grill, slice cheese thinly, or grate it, rather than using chunks.** Otherwise you'll have trouble getting the cheese fully melted before the bottom burns.

But our chunk recommendation doesn't apply to all cheeses. A good rule of thumb is: the firmer the cheese, the smaller the cheese morsel needed. Hard cheeses like Parmigiano-Reggiano and pecorino Romano need to be grated for pizza because they don't melt and flow like mozzarella and other medium-soft cheeses (see pages 10–13). If you use hard cheeses in chunks, you'll get partially melted lumps that are too firm for pizza, and may be too strongly flavored for one mouthful. Most medium-firm cheeses, like *manchego*, *Bra Duro*, and *ubriaco* give best results when coarsely grated. Soft or crumbly cheeses like feta and goat cheese don't flow when heated and need to be crumbled and distributed over the pizza.

"CAN I USE THE FREEZER TO SAVE EVEN MORE TIME?"

You can freeze our doughs anytime during their batch life, for up to three weeks. Make $1/2$-pound (orange-size) balls and wrap them well before freezing. Thaw overnight in the refrigerator and then use as usual. With the assistance of your freezer, there are three more ways to save even more time:

1. To freeze prepared $1/8$-inch-thick dough disks, line cookie sheets with parchment paper and freeze the prepared dough disks on the parchment. As soon as they're set (about 30 to 40 minutes), stack them, leaving parchment paper between disks. Pack into gallon-size ziplock bags, then freeze and use within three weeks. **Bake them still frozen** by placing, **unthawed,** on a greased baking sheet (see Chapter 3, Equipment, page 31), assembling the pizza, and then baking in a preheated oven. If you bake right on the parchment you can place it directly onto a preheated baking stone.

Visit PizzaIn5.com, where you'll find recipes, photos, videos, and instructional material. See page 53 for outdoor grill instructions.

2. To freeze a prebaked pizza crust: Bake the crusts "blind" (page XX), docking (puncturing) them well with a fork, and removing them from the oven when they just begin to brown (about 4 minutes). Check for puffing at 1 minute and dock again if you see any or you'll end up with pita bread. Allow to cool on a rack before separating crusts with parchment or wax paper and freezing in a ziplock bag. These will be far superior to store-bought prebaked pizza crusts, just as convenient, and a little quicker-baking than using unbaked frozen dough (see above). You can bake them frozen or defrosted (when using frozen crusts it will take a few more minutes to complete the baking).

3. To freeze a prebaked pizza: Bake a pizza as usual and allow it to cool completely. Freeze the pizza first on a cookie sheet, then, when frozen, put it into a heavy-duty freezer bag, preferably ziplock. When ready to use, remove from the bag, and place the pizza on a preheated baking stone for about 10 minutes (watch carefully to prevent scorching and consider a lower baking temperature if you're finding the pizza dry). While this method won't be quite as impressive as the other methods on this list, it's clearly the fastest.

"HOW CAN I USE FRESH GREENS ON PIZZA?"

American *pizzaioli* have been experimenting with fresh greens like arugula, often placed on top of the pizza *after* it's been baked. The result is a burst of fresh, bright, and cool flavor in every mouthful—the greens just barely wilt (and you get healthful green vegetables in the same bite as all that luscious cheese and other toppings). You can also bake the greens with the pizza—the most common form in this style is a spinach and cheese pizza, without tomato sauce (page 139). You can try baking the greens under the cheese, or if you want a drier, almost crispy effect, you can bake the greens on top of the cheese (page 129). We've enjoyed pizzas, in both styles, with arugula, watercress, spinach, and other leafy greens.

"HOW DO YOU BAKE PIZZA AND FLATBREAD ON A COVERED GAS GRILL?"

We love homemade pizza and flatbread so much that we refuse to give it up in the summertime. That presents a problem, because indoor oven-baked pizza uses a hot oven that heats up the house—which brings us to outdoor gas grills.

The first requirement is a *covered* grill; open grills can't approximate an oven so they don't do a good job on your toppings, though untopped pita breads (page 199) do well on an open grill.

Most modern gas grills that include a thermometer can accommodate our stored doughs. **We prefer gas grills over charcoal or wood-fired grills. Why?** The most important advantage of gas is its ability to control the heat. The trick in grilling dough is that you need the interior (crumb) to finish baking before the bottom chars. This is harder to do with charcoal or wood grills, including the heavy, covered, ceramic Japanese-style Kamado cookers. We have done it successfully, but since every charcoal grill is different, it's difficult for us to give standard instructions for charcoal and wood (see sidebar). So we tested our pizzas and flatbread on covered outdoor gas grills two ways:

∽

GRILLING PIZZA AND FLATBREAD OVER CHARCOAL OR WOOD: We've had success with charcoal and wood in a *covered* kettle-shaped grill. It's definitely trickier than the gas grill. Some tips:

1. Wait until flames have died down and you have hot embers for grilling.

2. Grill other dinner items first, or wait 15 to 20 minutes for the embers to partially cool by burning down. If the coals are red-hot, the pizzas tend to burn. Watch carefully until you know your grill well.

3. Depending on exactly how long you wait, you may need more time than we specify in our instructions for gas-grill pizza baking.

Visit PizzaIn5.com, where you'll find recipes, photos, videos, and instructional material. See page 53 for outdoor grill instructions.

DIRECT HEAT: All burners are lit, and at least some of the pizza is exposed to direct gas flame, creating a lovely rustic crunch.

INDIRECT HEAT: One or more burners are *un*-lit, so there are cool spots on the grate surface. Use cool spots to finish baking pizzas or flatbreads where there's been too much charring early on. For two-burner gas grills, you can stretch a narrow oval-shaped pizza that will fit between the two burners, allowing you to avoid direct heat completely when you want to.

- **Baking directly on the grates:** This gives the crunchiest, most rustic result, and adds smoky flavor to the pizza or flatbread. You can manipulate **direct and indirect heat** to finish the baking without burning the final product (see sidebar). Your grates should be clean and in good repair—a rough surface is much more likely to cause sticking. The dough will not fall in between the grates, even though it's very wet and flexible. You *must* first bake the crust "blind" (page 48) if you use this method.

- **Use a baking stone on the outdoor gas grill:** The results will be subtler, with less crunch, but it's much harder to burn things this way. This works best when all burners are switched on—that delivers the most even heat. Baking "blind" is optional with this method.

Let's start with a pizza or flatbread done right on the hot grates, in this case pita bread (page 199) or the basic pizza Master Recipe (Chapter 5, page 59). Pizza always starts life as a pita bread, if you think about it. Lean doughs (those made without eggs) are the ones that work best on the grill, because they're much more resistant to scorching and charring—eggs and sweetener can be used, but require lower gas settings and a closer eye (to a lesser extent, the same is true of doughs that are high in whole grains). Here's what you do:

1. Preheat the grill for 5 minutes, with the cover closed and all burners set to "high." Use a grill-cleaning brush to remove ash and debris.

2. Stretch the dough on a pizza peel or other floured work surface, to ⅛-inch thickness: Be persistent, because thicker ones will be more challenging to bake through without burning.

3. Bake it "blind," by lowering the heat settings for all burners to medium and sliding the dough round onto the center of the hot grate surface: You can thin out the dough a little more by allowing one end to slide onto the hot grate and then use your hand, as in the photo, to stretch a little more as you slide the board away. Parts of the dough round will be directly over gas flame. You don't need to oil the grates unless they are corroded. Assuming that they're smooth and clean, the floured dough will not stick. Close the lid and bake for about 3 minutes (try not to peek unless you smell burning), or until you see nice browning on the underside. Burner settings and timing will vary by grill and the fullness of your gas canister, so your unit may require higher or lower settings, or more or less time before flipping.

4. Flip the dough, using a large spatula, when it is puffy and the underside is browning—small areas may char. Bake another 3 minutes with the lid closed if this is pita bread, or *immediately* top with pizza sauces and cheese. Go easy on the toppings and you'll have less trouble getting them fully baked, and **always grate or slice cheese thinly rather than using chunks,**

Visit PizzaIn5.com, where you'll find recipes, photos, videos, and instructional material. See page 53 for outdoor grill instructions.

even if you're using medium-soft cheese. Most thin-crusted pizzas will need another 3 to 5 minutes on the second side, again with the lid closed (and again, try not to peek). **The trick is to get the toppings nicely melted before the underside chars; experiment with indirect heat to accomplish this (see sidebar, page 54). In grills that have "hot spots," that's the preferred approach.** It's difficult to get cheese to caramelize on outdoor grills—in most cases you'll have to settle for melted but not browned cheese, which is actually more like the way they serve it in Naples, Italy.

Pizza or flatbread can also be made on a baking stone placed on the grill grates. The Emile Henry Flame ceramic pizza stone is billed as being able to tolerate high grill heat, but other ceramic stones, or cast iron, work well, too. Let's use pita bread (page 199) and the basic pizza Master Recipe (Chapter 5, page 59) as examples. This method is a little more forgiving for enriched doughs (those made with eggs and usually sweetened) because the dough is more shielded from the intense and uneven heat of the gas flames. Especially if you turn down the burner heat (guided by your unit's built-in thermometer), you should be able to bake dessert flatbreads outside in the summertime by using a stone. Here's what you do:

1. Thirty minutes before grilling time, preheat a baking stone or cast-iron pan on an outdoor gas grill to the 450°F–500°F range (lower for enriched dough), with the grill cover closed. Try to achieve a near-constant temperature by regulating burner settings and monitoring the built-in thermometer. The temperature will vary and may only approximate what you get in an indoor oven. All burners should be on.

2. Stretch the dough on a pizza peel or other floured portable work surface, to ⅛-inch thickness: Be persistent, because thicker ones will be more challenging to bake through without burning. Make sure the dough round is moving well and not sticking to the board.

3. Top the pizza (unless this is pita): Go easy on the toppings and you'll have less trouble getting them fully baked and, again, **slice cheese thinly (or grate it) rather than using chunks, even if you're using medium-soft cheese.**

4. Slide the pizza onto the baking stone or into the cast-iron pan and bake, with the grill lid closed, for the recommended time. Be careful of burning and regulate the burner settings if the bottom is scorching. See the sidebar on page 54 for tips on using indirect heat to prevent burning.

Visit PizzaIn5.com, where you'll find recipes, photos, videos, and instructional material. See page 53 for outdoor grill instructions.

5

THE MASTER RECIPE

Classic Pizza Margherita

A detailed introduction to our simple method for making superfast pizza.

Thin-crusted *pizza Napoletana* (Neapolitan-Style Pizza) is our touchstone for great pizza. The standard version, with mozzarella, tomato, and basil, is known in Italy as *pizza Margherita* after Italy's Queen Margherita, for whom this patriotic pie with the three colors of the Italian flag was developed in 1889. It's crispy, thin, and delicious—that's a great way to start.

The crispiest crusts are baked right on a hot baking stone or a cast-iron pizza pan (see page 26), having been transferred there from a pizza peel. The secret to getting the pizza to slide right off the pizza peel and onto the stone is to minimize the time the dough spends sitting on the peel. That

∽

STEPS FROM TRADITIONAL ARTISAN BAKING THAT WE OMITTED:

1. Don't need to mix a new batch of dough every time we want pizza or flatbread.

2. Don't need to "proof" yeast.

3. Don't need to knead dough.

4. Don't need to fuss over doubling or tripling of dough volume.

5. Don't need to punch down and re-rise: **NEVER** punch down stored dough!

Now you know why it only takes five minutes a day, not including rising and baking time.

calls for one very strong recommendation: **Have all the toppings prepared and measured in advance.** Otherwise you will end up delaying at the crucial moment, and the dough might stick to the peel. Unfortunately, many of us who've made pizza know the result: When you try to slide the pizza into the oven, the dough is hesitant to slide off but the toppings aren't. Off they go to the back and bottom of the oven, which causes a smoky mess—and deep disappointment. If you really don't want to take a chance, you can bake pizza on a sheet of parchment paper, baking sheet, or heavy-duty half-sheet pan (see Chapter 4, page 47).

Makes enough dough for at least eight ½-pound pizzas or flatbreads (about 12 inches across). The recipe is easily doubled or halved.

INGREDIENT	VOLUME (U.S.)	WEIGHT (U.S.)	WEIGHT (METRIC)
Lukewarm water (100°F or below)	3½ cups	1 pound, 12 ounces	800 grams
Granulated yeast[1]	1 tablespoon	0.35 ounce	10 grams
Kosher salt[1]	1–1½ tablespoons	0.63–0.94 ounce	17–25 grams
Unbleached all-purpose flour	7½ cups (scoop and sweep)	2 pounds, 6 ounces	1,080 grams
Tomato topping of your choice (see page 109)	⅓ cup	3 ounces	85 grams
Fresh mozzarella, cut into ½-inch chunks	—	3 ounces	85 grams
6 fresh basil leaves, thinly slivered (see chiffonade technique, page 9), or torn			
Olive oil for drizzling over the pizza before baking			
Flour, cornmeal, or parchment paper for the pizza peel			

[1]Can decrease to taste (see pages 18 and 20).

VARIATION: Olive Oil Dough

Substitute ⅓ cup (2½ ounces/70 grams) of olive oil for ⅓ cup (2⅔ ounces/ 75 grams) of water, and the result is a marvelously flavorful, slightly richer pizza dough, or our preferred base for focaccia.

Mixing and Storing the Dough

1. **Warm the water slightly:** It should feel just a little warmer than body temperature, about 100°F. Using warm water will allow the dough to

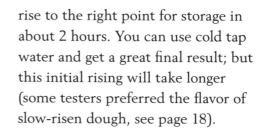

USE THE *SCOOP-AND-SWEEP* METHOD, NOT THE SPOON-AND-SWEEP METHOD: Our flour volume quantities are based on reaching into the flour bin with your measuring cup, scooping up a full measure all at once, and sweeping it level with a knife. Do not spoon flour bit by bit into the cup, which yields a much lighter cup and produces very wet dough that's impossible to handle.

rise to the right point for storage in about 2 hours. You can use cold tap water and get a great final result; but this initial rising will take longer (some testers preferred the flavor of slow-risen dough, see page 18).

2. **Add yeast and salt to the water** in a 5-quart bowl or, preferably, in a lidded (not airtight) plastic food container or food-grade bucket (see page 28). Don't worry about getting them to dissolve completely.

3. **Measure the flour with the "scoop-and-sweep" method or weigh the ingredients (see sidebars, pages 62 and 63). Then mix in the flour—kneading is unnecessary:** Add all of the flour and mix with a wooden spoon, Danish dough whisk (see page 30), 14-cup food processor (with dough attachment), or a heavy-duty stand mixer (with paddle).

You might need to use wet hands to get the last bit of flour to incorporate if you're not using a machine. **Don't knead; it isn't necessary.** You're finished when everything is uniformly moistened, without dry patches. This step is done in a matter of minutes, and yields dough that is loose enough to conform to the shape of its container.

4. **Allow to rise:** Cover with a non-airtight lid lid (see Equipment, pages 28–29). Allow the dough to rise at room temperature until it begins to flatten on the top, approximately 2 hours, depending on the room's temperature and the initial water temperature. **Do not punch down the dough!** With our method, you're trying to retain as much gas in the dough as possible, and punching it down knocks out gas and will make your pizzas and flatbreads dense.

5. **After rising, refrigerate and use over the next 14 days; the dough will develop sourdough characteristics over that time.** Fully refrigerated

WEIGHING YOUR INGREDIENTS: We've included equivalents for weight for this recipe. It's actually easier to weigh out ingredients rather than use cup measures. Consider using an electronic digital scale—simply press the "tare" (zeroing) button before adding an ingredient, then "tare" again to add the next.

> ⁓
>
> **FREEZER TECHNIQUES:** You can freeze the extra dough as dough balls, rolled-out disks, baked pizza shells, or even finished pies (page 51).

wet dough is less sticky and is easier to work with than dough at room temperature. So, the first time you try our method, it's best to refrigerate the dough overnight (or at least 3 hours) before use. Once it's refrigerated, the dough will collapse, and it will never rise again in the bucket—that's normal for our dough.

On Pizza Day

6. **Prepare and measure toppings in advance:** This will help you top the pizza quickly so you can get it into the oven before it sticks to the pizza peel.

7. **Thirty minutes before you're ready to bake, preheat a baking stone at your oven's highest temperature,** placed in the bottom third of the oven (consider a longer preheat if you're finding the crust results are too soft; see "Why Such a Short Preheat," page 49).

  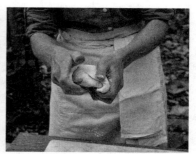

8. **Shape a ball in 20 to 30 seconds.** First, prepare a pizza peel with flour, cornmeal, or parchment paper to prevent your pizza from sticking to it when you slide it into the oven. Sprinkle the surface of your refrigerated dough with flour. Pull up and cut off a 1/2-pound (orange-size) piece of dough, using a serrated knife or kitchen shears. Hold the piece of dough in your hands and add a little more flour as needed so it won't stick to your hands. Gently stretch the surface of the dough around to the bottom on all four sides, rotating the dough a quarter-turn as you go to form a ball. Most of the dusting flour will fall off; it's not intended to be incorporated into the dough. The bottom of the ball may appear to be a collection of bunched ends, but it will flatten out and adhere when you roll it into a pizza or flatbread. The entire process should take no longer than 20 to 30 seconds.

9. **Roll out and stretch the pizza crust:** Flatten the dough with your hands and a rolling pin on a work surface or directly onto the pizza peel (or shape the disk by hand, see page 42) to produce a 1/8-inch-thick round, dusting

THROW THE PIZZA DOUGH UP IN THE AIR IF YOU'RE SO INCLINED. The secret is using the backs of your hands (the knuckles), not the fingertips. Gently toss up the well-floured and partly flattened dough while rotating your hands around each other. Rotate your dominant hand to a thumb-up position at the moment of lift-off (this gives you more control). Catch it on the backs of your hands (on the knuckles). This is best performed at outdoor pizza parties (see page 53 for grill directions). Don't try it with dough that's nearing the end of its storage life, as it tends to tear. The best throwing results, especially for beginners, are obtained with dough made with bread flour (page 75).

with flour to keep the dough from adhering to your work surface. A little sticking to the surface can be helpful in overcoming the dough's resistance to stretch. Use a dough scraper to unstick the dough as needed, and transfer it to the prepared pizza peel if you haven't already stretched the dough directly on one. (See Tips and Techniques, page 47, if you'd rather bake on a sheet pan). When you're finished, the dough round will be about 12 inches across, and should have enough flour under it to move easily when you shake the peel. As you add toppings, continue to test for sticking by gently shaking the peel. The pizza should move freely. If it doesn't, use the dough scraper and some flour to free it.

> ∽
>
> **PURISTS DO NOT ALLOW THE USE OF A ROLLING PIN (AND NEITHER DO ITALIAN GOVERNMENT REGULATIONS), BUT YOU HAVE OUR PERMISSION**. We've used rolling pins for years—if you want to try hand-stretching the dough, see page 42.

10. **Add the toppings:** Spread the tomato topping over the dough, leaving a ½-inch border at the edges, then add the cheese and basil (for a different effect, put the basil on *after* baking). We prefer using well-spaced chunks of cheese, which gradually melt and spread

(giving the crust a longer opportunity to crisp before the toppings burn). Drizzle a little olive oil over the pizza if desired.

11. **Slide the pizza onto the preheated stone:** Place the tip of the peel near the back of the stone, close to where you want the far edge of the pizza to land. Give the peel a few quick forward-and-back jiggles and pull it sharply out from under the pizza (if you're using a sheet pan, place it right on the stone). Check for doneness in 8 to 10 minutes, and turn the pizza around in the oven if one side is browning faster than the other. It may take up to 5 minutes more in the oven. Using a spatula may be helpful in getting the baked pizza back onto the peel.

Visit PizzaIn5.com, where you'll find recipes, photos, videos, and instructional material. See page 53 for outdoor grill instructions.

Allow to cool slightly, preferably on a wire cooling rack, so that the cheese sets. *Buon appetito!*

12. **Store the remaining dough in the refrigerator in your lidded (not airtight) container and use it over the next 14 days:** You'll find that even one day's storage improves the flavor, texture, and the color of pizza and flatbread crusts. The dough begins to ferment and take on sourdough characteristics. Cut off and shape more dough as you need it. The dough can also be frozen in $1/2$-pound portions in an airtight container for up to 3 weeks; defrost overnight in the refrigerator prior to baking day. This is a particularly nice option for an egg-enriched dough, which has a 5-day refrigerator life (see Chapter 10, page 251).

VARIATION: Pizza Marinara (Sailor's Pizza)

It doesn't get any easier than this—pizza marinara is nothing but a Margherita pizza without mozzarella or basil. You can use a little slivered or crushed garlic, an olive oil drizzle, and oregano if you like, or even some grated Parmigiano-Reggiano, but they're all optional.

VARIATION: Superthin Pizza/Cracker Crust (see Tips and Techniques, page 42)

For a superthin crust, use half as much dough ($1/4$ pound, about the size of a peach). Roll it out very thinly, to about $1/16$ inch, and use 25 percent less topping

---

∽

ATTENTION LAZY PEOPLE: So long as your dough doesn't have eggs, dairy, or other perishables, you don't need to wash the mixing and storage vessel between batches. The leftover dough jump-starts the sourdough process and imparts a rich flavor to the new batch (you can include up to $1/2$ cups of "old" dough).

so the thin crust isn't weighed down. Grate your cheese rather than using chunks. The baking temperature remains the same, but you will likely need less time, so check for doneness after about 5 minutes. If you're not getting the crispy result you're looking for, consider baking the crust "blind" (see page 48).

VARIATION: Mushroom Pizza

Toss together 1 cup thinly sliced mushrooms (button, portobello, shiitake, or any of your favorites) with 1 tablespoon olive oil, a pinch of salt and pepper, and ½ teaspoon chopped fresh thyme. Cover the rolled-out dough with ⅓ cup of tomato sauce (page 9) and 3 ounces of mozzarella or fontina cheese, and top with the mushrooms. Bake as directed.

VARIATION: Sausage Pizza

"One night my eleven-year-old son made a sausage pizza. He skipped the step of cooking the sausage first, because he is eleven and not eager to create more work for himself. He put small pieces of the raw sausage all over the pizza and baked it. The result was amazing, perfectly cooked sausage."—Zoë

Cover the rolled-out dough with ⅓ cup of tomato sauce (page 9), 3 ounces of mozzarella or fontina cheese, and top with 1 large, raw sausage cut into ¼-inch pieces. Bake as directed.

Visit PizzaIn5.com, where you'll find recipes, photos, videos, and instructional material. See page 53 for outdoor grill instructions.

6

MORE DOUGHS AND GREAT SAVORY SAUCES

Crisp-Yet-Tender Pizza Dough Even Closer to the Style of Naples

In Italy, Neapolitan pizza is made with flour that's lower in protein than what you find in North American unbleached all-purpose white flour. In Naples, *pizzaioli* start with Italian "00" flour, which is a lower-protein product, but they kick up the protein by adding a little high-protein bread flour (often a North American import). These "00" flours are available through the Internet or mail order in the United States (see Ingredients, page 5), but bleached all-purpose flour is a little lower in protein than unbleached and makes a good substitute. Since it's one of the most commonly available flours, we used it here in our primary Naples formula, with variations using low-protein cake flour, and another using "00" for people willing to seek it out.

Lower protein creates a very light crust that is crispy, tender on the inside, and never tough. At the edges, where there is more puffing, you can really appreciate the tender interior. If everything is just so, the crumb should melt in your mouth.

Makes enough dough for at least eight ¹/₂-pound pizzas (about 12 inches across). The recipe is easily doubled or halved.

INGREDIENT	VOLUME (U.S.)	WEIGHT (U.S.)	WEIGHT (METRIC)
Lukewarm water	4³⁄₄ cups	1 pound, 14 ounces	845 grams
Granulated yeast[1]	1 tablespoon	0.35 ounce	10 grams
Kosher salt[1]	1–1¹⁄₂ tablespoons	0.63–0.94 ounce	17–25 grams
Bleached all-purpose flour	8 cups	2 pounds, 8 ounces	1135 grams

[1]Can decrease to taste (see pages 18 and 20).

1. **Mixing and storing the dough:** Mix the yeast and salt with the water in a 5-quart bowl, or a lidded (not airtight) food container.

2. Mix in the flour without kneading, using a spoon, a 14-cup food processor (with dough attachment), or a heavy-duty stand mixer (with paddle). If you're not using a machine, you may need to use wet hands to incorporate the last bit of flour.

3. Cover (not airtight), and allow it to rest at room temperature until the dough rises and collapses (or flattens on top), approximately 2 hours.

4. The dough can be used immediately after its initial rise, though it is easier to handle when cold. Refrigerate it in a lidded (not airtight) container and use for pizza or flatbread over the next 14 days. The flavor will be best if you wait for at least 24 hours of refrigeration.

Or store the dough for up to 3 weeks in the freezer in 1/2-pound portions. When using frozen dough, thaw it in the refrigerator overnight before use.

5. **On pizza or flatbread day,** roll out or stretch the dough into a thin round and finish with your favorite toppings, using any of the recipes in this book.

VARIATION: The Ultimate Tender Neapolitan Crust
If you really want to make the pizza of Naples, you need Italian-style low-protein flour, or re-create it with a mixture of all-purpose and cake flour. For either version, chill the dough for 3 hours after the initial rise, or the dough will be a bit too sticky.

"OO" FLOUR: CAPUTO, OR KING ARTHUR ITALIAN-STYLE FLOUR (SEE SOURCES, PAGE 281)			
INGREDIENT	VOLUME (U.S.)	WEIGHT (U.S.)	WEIGHT (METRIC)
Lukewarm water	3 cups	1 pound, 8 ounces	680 grams
Granulated yeast[1]	1 tablespoon	0.35 ounce	10 grams
Kosher salt[1]	1-1 1/2 tablespoons	0.63–0.94 ounce	17–25 grams
"OO" flour	7 1/2 cups	2 pounds, 2 ounces	960 grams

[1]Can decrease to taste (see pages 18 and 20).

Visit PizzaIn5.com, where you'll find recipes, photos, videos, and instructional material. See page 53 for outdoor grill instructions.

50/50 ALL-PURPOSE AND CAKE FLOUR

BY USING CAKE FLOUR (WHICH IS LOW IN PROTEIN), THIS COMBINATION WILL ACHIEVE A SIMILAR RESULT TO WHAT YOU GET WITH ITALIAN "00."

INGREDIENT	VOLUME (U.S.)	WEIGHT (U.S.)	WEIGHT (METRIC)
Lukewarm water	3¼ cups	1 pound, 10 ounces	740 grams
Granulated yeast[1]	1 tablespoon	0.35 ounce	10 grams
Kosher salt[1]	1–1½ tablespoons	0.63–0.94 ounce	17–25 grams
Unbleached all-purpose flour	4 cups	1 pound, 4 ounces	570 grams
Cake flour	4 cups	1 pound	455 grams

[1]Can decrease to taste (see pages 18 and 20).

Pizza Dough for Throwing

Throwing and spinning dough into the air isn't necessary, but it's fun, especially when people get together for pizza parties, preferably outdoors (see page 53).

Strong Dough Needs Stronger Flour: Bread flour, which is higher in protein, is sometimes called "strong" flour (especially in British recipes). This is because dough made with higher-protein flour is more resilient and elastic—it actually does feel stronger, and it's more resistant to tearing than doughs made from all-purpose flour.

This higher-protein flour can toughen cakes, biscuits, and other light baked goods, but not pizza. Extra resiliency can be helpful if you're planning to throw your pizza dough into the air, or if you prefer a chewier crust. While we often throw pizzas made with all-purpose flour, they're a little more prone to tearing. This stronger, more resilient pizza dough works particularly well in thicker American-style pizza, but it's also great for thin crusts—it may take a little longer than usual to get it really thin. Be patient with it, and try your hand at throwing it in the air (see page 65).

Makes enough dough for at least eight ¹/₂-pound pizzas or flatbreads (about 12 inches across). The recipe is easily doubled or halved.

INGREDIENT	VOLUME (U.S.)	WEIGHT (U.S.)	WEIGHT (METRIC)
Lukewarm water	3 cups	1 pound, 8 ounces	680 grams
Granulated yeast[1]	1 tablespoon	0.35 ounce	10 grams
Kosher salt[1]	1–1½ tablespoons	0.63–0.94 ounce	17–25 grams
Sugar, honey, malt powder, or agave syrup	1 tablespoon	—	—
Olive oil	⅛ cup	1 ounce	30 grams
Bread flour (sometimes labeled "high-protein" or "strong" flour)	7 cups	2 pounds, 3 ounces	995 grams

[1]Can decrease to taste (see pages 18 and 20).

1. **Mixing and storing the dough:** Mix the yeast, salt, sweetener, and olive oil with the water in a 5-quart bowl, or a lidded (not airtight) food container.

2. Mix in the flour without kneading, using a spoon, a 14-cup food processor (with dough attachment), or a heavy-duty stand mixer (with paddle). If you're not using a machine, you may need to use wet hands to incorporate the last bit of flour.

3. Cover (not airtight), and allow it to rest at room temperature until the dough rises and collapses (or flattens on top), approximately 2 hours.

4. The dough can be used immediately after its initial rise, though it is easier to handle when cold. Refrigerate it in a lidded (not airtight) container and use for pizza or flatbread over the next 14 days. Or store the dough for up to 3 weeks in the freezer in ½-pound portions. When using frozen dough, thaw it in the refrigerator overnight before use.

5. **On pizza or flatbread day,** roll out or stretch the dough into a thin round and finish with your favorite toppings, using any of the recipes in this book.

Visit PizzaIn5.com, where you'll find recipes, photos, videos, and instructional material. See page 53 for outdoor grill instructions.

American-Style Pizza Dough

"Kids love the crust on fast-food American pizza, which tends to be softer—almost fluffy—and a little sweet. By adding whole, low-fat, or skim milk and a touch of sugar to our basic recipe we get just that sensation. When we make pizza with this dough the kids eat every last bite, including the crust. And I'll confess, we parents love it too. It is equally good in a thin- or thick-crust pie."—Zoë

Makes enough dough for at least eight ¹/₂-pound pizzas or flatbreads (about 12 inches across). The recipe is easily doubled or halved.

INGREDIENT	VOLUME (U.S.)	WEIGHT (U.S.)	WEIGHT (METRIC)
Lukewarm milk	3¹/₄ cups	1 pound, 12 ounces	795 grams
Granulated yeast[1]	1 tablespoon	0.35 ounce	10 grams
Kosher salt[1]	1-1¹/₂ tablespoons	0.63–0.94 ounce	17–25 grams
Sugar	3 tablespoons	1¹/₂ ounces	42 grams
Neutral-flavored oil	¹/₄ cup	2 ounces	56 grams
Unbleached all-purpose flour	7 cups	2 pounds, 3 ounces	995 grams

[1]Can decrease to taste (see pages 18 and 20).

1. **Mixing and storing the dough:** Mix the yeast, salt, sugar, and oil with the milk in a 5-quart bowl, or a lidded (not airtight) food container.

2. Mix in the flour without kneading, using a spoon, a 14-cup capacity food processor (with dough attachment), or a heavy-duty stand mixer (with paddle). If you're not using a machine, you may need to use wet hands to incorporate the last bit of flour.

3. Cover (not airtight), and allow it to rest at room temperature until the dough rises and collapses (or flattens on top), approximately 2 hours.

4. The dough can be used immediately after its initial rise, though it is easier to handle when cold. Refrigerate it in a lidded (not airtight) container and use over the next 7 days. Or store the dough for up to 3 weeks in the freezer in ½-pound portions. When using frozen dough, thaw it in the refrigerator overnight before use.

5. **On pizza or flatbread day,** roll out or stretch the dough into a thin round and finish with your favorite toppings, using any of the recipes in this book.

Semolina Dough

The heavenly flavor and vibrant yellow color of semolina appear in typical Italian sesame loaves, but rarely in pizza. We think that's a shame, since semolina dough creates a lovely rustic and chewy effect when baked flat, and gives the crust a sweetness and an almost-winey aroma. The best semolina for bread is finely ground and labeled as "durum flour." It is available from Bob's Red Mill in groceries or through the Internet or mail order from King Arthur Flour (page 281).

Makes enough dough for at least eight ¹/₂-pound pizzas or flatbreads (about 12 inches across). The recipe is easily doubled or halved.

INGREDIENT	VOLUME (U.S.)	WEIGHT (U.S.)	WEIGHT (METRIC)
Lukewarm water	3 cups	1 pound, 8 ounces	680 grams
Granulated yeast[1]	1 tablespoon	0.35 ounce	10 grams
Kosher salt[1]	1–1½ tablespoons	0.63–0.94 ounce	17–25 grams
Durum flour	3 cups	1 pound, 2 ounces	510 grams
Unbleached all-purpose flour	3¼ cups	1 pound	455 grams

[1]Can decrease to taste (see pages 18 and 20).

1. **Mixing and storing the dough:** Mix the yeast and salt with the water in a 5-quart bowl, or a lidded (not airtight) food container.

2. Mix in the flours without kneading, using a spoon, a 14-cup capacity food processor (with dough attachment), or a heavy-duty stand mixer (with paddle). If you're not using a machine, you may need to use wet hands to incorporate the last bit of flour.

3. Cover (not airtight), and allow it to rest at room temperature until the dough rises and collapses (or flattens on top), approximately 2 hours.

4. The dough can be used immediately after its initial rise, though it is easier to handle when cold. Refrigerate it in a lidded (not airtight) container and use for pizza or flatbread over the next 14 days. The flavor will be best if you wait for at least 24 hours of refrigeration. Or store the dough for up to 3 weeks in the freezer in ½-pound portions. When using frozen dough, thaw it in the refrigerator overnight before use.

5. **On pizza or flatbread day,** roll out or stretch the dough into a thin round and finish with your favorite toppings, using any of the recipes in this book.

Visit PizzaIn5.com, where you'll find recipes, photos, videos, and instructional material. See page 53 for outdoor grill instructions.

100% Whole Wheat Dough

White whole wheat, lighter in color and milder in flavor than traditional whole wheat, has been a marvelous addition to groceries in the last decade. Great products are now available from King Arthur Flour, Hodgson Mill, and Bob's Red Mill. Use it whenever you want the goodness of whole wheat with a less assertive flavor than traditional whole wheat.

This recipe can also be made with half whole wheat and half unbleached all-purpose, for a lighter result (see variation below).

Makes enough dough for at least eight ¹/₂-pound pizzas or flatbreads (about 12 inches across). The recipe is easily doubled or halved.

INGREDIENT	VOLUME (U.S.)	WEIGHT (U.S.)	WEIGHT (METRIC)
Lukewarm water	3¹/₂ cups	1 pound, 12 ounces	795 grams
Granulated yeast[1]	1 tablespoon	0.35 ounce	10 grams
Kosher salt[1]	1–1¹/₂ tablespoons	0.63–0.94 ounce	17–25 grams
Sugar, honey, malt powder, or agave syrup	2 tablespoons	—	—
Olive oil	¹/₈ cup	1 ounce	30 grams
White whole wheat flour (or traditional whole wheat)	7 cups	2 pounds	900 grams

[1]Can decrease to taste (see pages 18 and 20).

1. **Mixing and storing the dough:** Mix the yeast, salt, sweetener, and olive oil with the water in a 5-quart bowl, or a lidded (not airtight) food container.

2. Mix in the remaining dry ingredients without kneading, using a spoon, a 14-cup capacity food processor (with dough attachment), or a heavy-duty stand mixer (with paddle). If you're not using a machine, you may need to use wet hands to incorporate the last bit of flour.

3. Cover (not airtight), and allow it to rest at room temperature until the dough rises and collapses (or flattens on top), approximately 2 hours.

4. The dough can be used immediately after its initial rise, though it is easier to handle when cold. Refrigerate it in a lidded (not airtight) container and use for pizza or flatbread over the next 7 days. Or store the dough for up to 3 weeks in the freezer in ½-pound portions. When using frozen dough, thaw it in the refrigerator overnight before use.

5. **On pizza or flatbread day,** roll out or stretch the dough into a thin round and finish with your favorite toppings, using any of the recipes in this book.

VARIATION: Lighter Whole Wheat Dough

For a lighter dough, use half whole wheat and half unbleached all-purpose, decreasing the water to 3¼ cups. This dough retains its lightness in the refrigerator and can be stored a bit longer (10 days).

Visit PizzaIn5.com, where you'll find recipes, photos, videos, and instructional material. See page 53 for outdoor grill instructions.

100% Whole Grain Spelt Dough

Spelt is an ancient grain, a variety of wheat that is lower in gluten and less bitter than standard wheat—the effect is closer to white whole wheat (see page 82). The flavor is hearty, and the crust is more tender than crusts made with white dough. If you're trying to add more whole grain to your family's diet, this can be a great way to get picky eaters to try something new.

Makes enough dough for at least eight ¹/₂-pound pizzas or flatbreads (about 12 inches across). The recipe is easily doubled or halved.

INGREDIENT	VOLUME (U.S.)	WEIGHT (U.S.)	WEIGHT (METRIC)
Lukewarm water	3¹/₄ cups	1 pound 10 ounces	735 grams
Granulated yeast[1]	1 tablespoon	0.35 ounce	10 grams
Kosher salt[1]	1–1¹/₂ tablespoons	0.63–0.94 ounce	17–25 grams
Sugar, honey, malt powder, or agave syrup	2 tablespoons	—	—
Olive oil	¹/₈ cup	1 ounce	30 grams
Whole grain spelt flour	8 cups	2 pounds, 4 ounces	1,040 grams

[1]Can decrease to taste (see pages 18 and 20).

1. **Mixing and storing the dough:** Mix the yeast, salt, sweetener, and olive oil with the water in a 5-quart bowl, or a lidded (not airtight) food container.

2. Mix in the remaining dry ingredients without kneading, using a spoon, a 14-cup capacity food processor (with dough attachment), or a heavy-duty stand mixer (with paddle). If you're not using a machine, you may need to use wet hands to incorporate the last bit of flour.

3. Cover (not airtight), and allow it to rest at room temperature until the dough rises and collapses (or flattens on top), approximately 2 hours.

4. The dough can be used immediately after its initial rise, though it is easier to handle when cold. Refrigerate it in a lidded (not airtight) container and use for pizza or flatbread over the next 7 days. Or store the dough for up to 3 weeks in the freezer in $1/2$-pound portions. When using frozen dough, thaw it in the refrigerator overnight before use.

5. **On pizza or flatbread day,** roll out or stretch the dough into a thin round and finish with your favorite toppings, using any of the recipes in this book.

VARIATION: Half-Spelt Dough
For a lighter result, you can use half spelt and half unbleached all-purpose flour. Everything else stays the same.

Visit PizzaIn5.com, where you'll find recipes, photos, videos, and instructional material. See page 53 for outdoor grill instructions.

Cornmeal Olive Oil Dough

We developed this dough specifically for the Chicago-Style Deep-Dish Pizza (page 191), but discovered that its light corn flavor is delicious in our other recipes; kids love it with all kinds of toppings.

Makes enough dough for at least eight ¹/₂-pound pizzas or flatbreads (about 12 inches across). The recipe is easily doubled or halved.

INGREDIENT	VOLUME (U.S.)	WEIGHT (U.S.)	WEIGHT (METRIC)
Lukewarm water	2¾ cups	1 pound, 6 ounces	625 grams
Granulated yeast[1]	1 tablespoon	0.35 ounce	10 grams
Kosher salt[1]	1–1½ tablespoons	0.63–0.94 ounce	17–25 grams
Sugar, honey, malt powder, or agave syrup	3 tablespoons	—	—
Olive oil	¾ cup	6 ounces	165 grams
Unbleached all-purpose flour	6 cups	1 pound, 14 ounces	850 grams
Yellow cornmeal	¾ cup	4 ounces	125 grams

[1]Can decrease to taste (see pages 18 and 20).

1. **Mixing and storing the dough:** Mix the yeast, salt, and sweetener with the water and olive oil in a 5-quart bowl, or a lidded (not airtight) food container.

2. Mix in the remaining dry ingredients without kneading, using a spoon, a 14-cup capacity food processor (with dough attachment), or a heavy-duty stand mixer (with paddle). If you're not using a machine, you may need to use wet hands to incorporate the last bit of flour.

3. Cover (not airtight), and allow it to rest at room temperature until the dough rises and collapses (or flattens on top), approximately 2 hours.

4. The dough can be used immediately after its initial rise, though it is easier to handle when cold. Refrigerate it in a lidded (not airtight) container and use over the next 10 days. Or store the dough for up to 3 weeks in the freezer in $^1/_2$-pound portions. When using frozen dough, thaw it in the refrigerator overnight before use.

5. **On pizza or flatbread day,** roll out or stretch the dough into a round and finish with your favorite toppings, using any of the recipes in this book.

Visit PizzaIn5.com, where you'll find recipes, photos, videos, and instructional material. See page 53 for outdoor grill instructions.

Naan Dough

This dough is made with milk and yogurt, so it has a tenderness and slight tang that we love. It can be baked plain and slathered with ghee (clarified butter) or topped with garlic and herbs. For a heartier version try the dough stuffed with savory fillings (page 224).

Makes enough dough for at least eight ½-pound naans, pizzas, or flatbreads. The recipe is easily doubled or halved.

INGREDIENT	VOLUME (U.S.)	WEIGHT (U.S.)	WEIGHT (METRIC)
Lukewarm water	1½ cups	12 ounces	340 grams
Lukewarm milk (whole, low-fat, or nonfat)	1½ cups	12 ounces	340 grams
Granulated yeast[1]	1 tablespoon	0.35 ounce	10 grams
Kosher salt[1]	1–1½ tablespoons	0.63–0.94 ounce	17–25 grams
Yogurt (whole, low-fat, or nonfat)	½ cup	4½ ounces	125 grams
Sugar, honey, malt powder, or agave syrup	2 tablespoons	—	—
Unbleached all-purpose flour	7 cups	2 pounds, 3 ounces	990 grams

[1]Can decrease to taste (see pages 18 and 20).

1. **Mixing and storing the dough:** Mix the yeast, salt, yogurt, and sweetener with the water and milk in a 5-quart bowl, or a lidded (not airtight) food container.

2. Mix in the remaining dry ingredients without kneading, using a spoon, a 14-cup capacity food processor (with dough attachment), or a heavy-duty stand mixer (with paddle). If you're not using a machine, you may need to use wet hands to incorporate the last bit of flour.

3. Cover (not airtight), and allow it to rest at room temperature until the dough rises and collapses (or flattens on top), approximately 2 hours.

4. The dough can be used immediately after its initial rise, though it is easier to handle when cold. Refrigerate it in a lidded (not airtight) container and use for pizza or flatbread over the next 7 days. Or store the dough for up to 3 weeks in the freezer in $1/2$-pound portions. When using frozen dough, thaw it in the refrigerator overnight before use.

5. **On pizza or flatbread day,** roll out or stretch the dough into a thin round and finish with your favorite toppings, using any of the recipes in this book.

Visit PizzaIn5.com, where you'll find recipes, photos, videos, and instructional material. See page 53 for outdoor grill instructions.

Corn Masa Dough

Corn was grown in both the northern and southern hemispheres by Native Americans. In Mexico and in Central and South America, whole civilizations were able to live on it because it was treated with alkali minerals ("lime") before use, creating corn masa, which has a wonderful distinctive flavor. The alkali released niacin, an essential B vitamin, preventing a host of deficiency diseases and allowing pre-Columbian societies to thrive.

Masa dough is usually made into unleavened tortillas (see page 103). Our adaptation calls for wheat flour to turn masa into a yeasted flatbread. Use with your favorite Mexican or Southwestern toppings, or try our version on page 229. It also makes a great traditional European-style pizza.

If you can't get corn masa flour (masa harina) where you live, substitute cornmeal. The flavor will be less distinctive but still delicious.

Makes enough dough for at least eight $^{1}/_{2}$-pound pizzas or flatbreads (about 12 inches across). The recipe is easily doubled or halved.

1. **Mixing and storing the dough:** Mix the yeast, salt, sweetener, and oil with the water in a 5-quart bowl, or a lidded (not airtight) food container.

2. Mix in the dry ingredients without kneading, using a spoon, a 14-cup capacity food processor (with dough attachment), or a heavy-duty stand mixer (with paddle). If you're not using a machine, you may need to use wet hands to incorporate the last bit of flour.

INGREDIENT	VOLUME (U.S.)	WEIGHT (U.S.)	WEIGHT (METRIC)
Lukewarm water	3 cups	1 pound, 8 ounces	680 grams
Granulated yeast[1]	1 tablespoon	0.35 ounce	10 grams
Kosher salt[1]	1–1½ tablespoons	0.63–0.94 ounce	17–25 grams
Sugar, honey, malt powder, or agave syrup	1 tablespoon	—	—
Neutral-flavored oil	⅛ cup	1 ounce	30 grams
Corn masa flour (masa harina)	1½ cups	13 ounces	365 grams
Unbleached all-purpose flour	5 cups	1 pound, 9 ounces	710 grams

[1]Can decrease to taste (see pages 18 and 20).

3. Cover (not airtight), and allow it to rest at room temperature until the dough rises and collapses (or flattens on top), approximately 2 hours.

4. The dough can be used immediately after its initial rise, though it is easier to handle when cold. Refrigerate it in a lidded (not airtight) container and use for pizza or flatbread over the next 10 days. Or store the dough for up to 3 weeks in the freezer in ½-pound portions. When using frozen dough, thaw it in the refrigerator overnight before use.

5. **On pizza or flatbread day,** roll out or stretch the dough into a thin round and finish with your favorite toppings, using any of the recipes in this book.

VARIATION: Substitute 1½ cups regular cornmeal (yellow or white) for corn masa flour.

VARIATION: Dough for Spicy Jalapeño Cheese Breadsticks
Add 1 tablespoon minced seeded jalapeño pepper and 1 cup grated cheddar cheese with the liquid in Step 1. Use the dough within 7 days to make thick bread sticks following the directions on page 248, or the thin crispy ones below.

VARIATION: Thin Crispy Bread Sticks
To make thin crispy bread sticks, follow the directions below:

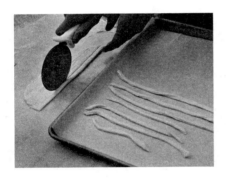

1. Preheat the oven to 400°F. Roll out the dough into an 8 by 13-inch rectangle, ⅛ inch thick, then cut ⅛-inch-wide strips with a pizza cutter or sharp knife.

2. Lay the strips out on a baking sheet prepared with oil, butter, or parchment paper, leaving ½ inch between each strip. Using a pastry brush, daub olive oil over each strip and sprinkle with coarse salt.

3. Bake the bread sticks near the center of the oven for 10 to 16 minutes, depending on thickness and width. The bread sticks are done when nicely browned and beginning to crisp; they will firm up when cool.

Rustic and Hearty Rye Dough

People usually associate rye flour with the bread-loving cultures of Eastern Europe and Russia, but rye flour also lends a terrific rustic quality to Mediterranean flatbreads and pizzas. **For a superfast version of deli rye bread, make a pita bread from this dough, then brush with water and sprinkle with caraway seeds just before baking (see Variation: Pita, page 201).** Stuff caraway rye pitas with corned beef or pastrami and a dollop of hearty brown mustard, and serve with a dill pickle on the side.

Makes enough dough for at least eight ¹/₂-pound pizzas or flatbreads (about 12 inches across). The recipe is easily doubled or halved.

INGREDIENT	VOLUME (U.S.)	WEIGHT (U.S.)	WEIGHT (METRIC)
Lukewarm water (100°F or below)	3¹/₄ cups	1 pound, 10 ounces	740 grams
Granulated yeast[1]	1 tablespoon	0.35 ounce	10 grams
Kosher salt[1]	1–1¹/₂ tablespoons	0.63–0.94 ounce	17–25 grams
Neutral-flavored oil, or olive oil	¹/₄ cup	2 ounces	55 grams
Rye flour	1¹/₂ cups	6¹/₂ ounces	185 grams
Unbleached all-purpose flour	6 cups	1 pound, 14 ounces	850 grams

[1]Can decrease to taste (see pages 18 and 20).

1. **Mixing and storing the dough:** Mix the yeast, salt, and oil with the water in a 5-quart bowl, or a lidded (not airtight) food container.

2. Mix in the flours without kneading, using a spoon, a 14-cup capacity food processor (with dough attachment), or a heavy-duty stand mixer (with paddle). If you're not using a machine, you may need to use wet hands to incorporate the last bit of flour.

3. Cover (not airtight), and allow it to rest at room temperature until the dough rises and collapses (or flattens on top), approximately 2 hours.

4. The dough can be used immediately after its initial rise, though it is easier to handle when cold. Refrigerate it in a lidded (not airtight) container and use for pizza or flatbread over the next 10 days. Or store the dough for up to 2 weeks in the freezer in $^1/_2$-pound portions. When using frozen dough, thaw it in the refrigerator overnight before use.

5. **On pizza or flatbread day,** roll out or stretch the dough into thin rounds and finish with your favorite toppings, using any of the recipes in this book.

VARIATION: *Knekkebrød* (100% Whole Grain Rye Dough)

To re-create the hearty whole grain crackers and flatbreads of Scandinavia (pages 234 and 236), use this 100% whole grain rye variation. It can even be used to make all sorts of very nontraditional pizzas. Don't expect a lot of airiness or rise from this dough, and don't be alarmed if it seems to be just sitting there in the bucket—the yeast gives it just enough lift, but you won't see much rising. Don't try to make a thick *knekkebrød* crust, or it will be very doughy. It's best at $^1/_{16}$-inch thickness maximum, and a paper-thin version is sublime (page 42). It's a bit challenging to get the fragile dough this thin, but be patient—it's worth it. The easiest way to achieve this thickness is to use the rolling instructions for the gluten-free dough on page 96.

The dough is identical to the Rustic and Hearty Rye Dough, except add ⅛ cup sugar, honey, malt powder, or agave syrup to the water, omit the white flour, and use 8 cups whole grain rye dough. Stores for 5 days.

Gluten-Free Pizza and Flatbread Dough

This makes a delicious, tender, and crispy crust, which works for all of our pizza and flatbread recipes. We developed it for those who crave pizza but can't tolerate gluten. Even those of us who can will love this dough.

Makes enough dough for at least eight ¹/₂-pound pizzas or flatbreads (about 12 inches across). The recipe is easily doubled or halved.

INGREDIENT	VOLUME (U.S.)	WEIGHT (U.S.)	WEIGHT (METRIC)
Brown rice flour	2 cups	11 ounces	320 grams
White rice flour	2 cups	10	280 grams
Tapioca flour ("starch")	2 cups	9 ounces	265 grams
Cornmeal	1 ½ cups	9 ounces	265 grams
Granulated yeast	2 tablespoons	0.75 ounce	20 grams
Kosher salt[1]	1–1½ tablespoons	0.63–0.94 ounce	17–25 grams
Xanthan gum	2 tablespoons	½ ounce	18 grams
Lukewarm water	3¼ cups	1 pound, 10 ounces	730 grams
Olive oil	½ cup	4 ounces	110 grams
Eggs, large, lightly beaten (see substitute, page 97)	2	4 ounces	110 grams

[1]Can decrease to taste (see page 20).

(continued)

INGREDIENT	VOLUME (U.S.)	WEIGHT (U.S.)	WEIGHT (METRIC)
Sugar, honey, malt powder, or agave syrup	2 tablespoons	—	—

1. **Mixing and storing the dough:** Whisk together the flours, cornmeal, yeast, salt, and xanthan gum in a 5-quart bowl, or a lidded (not airtight) food container.

2. Combine the liquid ingredients with the sweetener and add the mixture to the dry ingredients, using a spoon, 14-cup food processor (with dough attachment), or a heavy-duty stand mixer (with paddle), until all of the dry ingredients are well incorporated. You may have to use wet hands to get the last bit of flour to incorporate if you're not using a machine.

EGG SUBSTITUTE: If you're avoiding eggs, swap 1 tablespoon finely ground flaxseed mixed with 3 tablespoons water for each egg.

3. Cover (not airtight), and allow it to rest at room temperature until the dough rises, approximately 2 hours.

4. The dough can be used immediately after its initial rise, though it is easier to handle when cold. Refrigerate it in a lidded (not airtight) container and use over the next 5 days. Or store the dough for up to

3 weeks in the freezer in ½-pound portions. When using frozen dough, thaw it in the refrigerator overnight before use.

5. **On pizza or flatbread day,** break off a piece of dough. It will not have any stretchiness like wheat doughs. Roll out the dough directly on a pizza peel, covered generously with rice flour. Sprinkle the surface of the dough with a little more rice flour and cover the dough with plastic wrap. Roll into a ⅛-inch-thick round. As you roll out the dough, use a dough scraper to make sure the dough isn't sticking to the peel; add more flour if needed. Gently pull off the plastic wrap, and finish with your favorite toppings, using many of the recipes in this book. See sidebar, page 104, for more rolling instructions.

Chapati (Non-Yeasted Whole Wheat Dough)

"I first learned this technique from my friend chef Suvir Saran. He made a whole wheat dough, rolled a thin, perfectly round disk and then barely cooked it in an iron skillet before he threw it over an open flame where it puffed into a sphere. It was a thrill to see this dough in action."—Zoë

Traditionally, chapati dough is not yeasted. It goes together in a snap and has a wonderful toasted flavor. This dough can be mixed, rolled out, and cooked in less than five minutes, the fastest bread in the book. See the recipes following this for equally fast flour and corn tortillas.

You can also use the same cooking technique with our yeasted doughs. The trick is to roll it as thin and as round as you can, although we don't achieve this shape every time and it still seems to work.

Makes about six 6-inch chapatis. The recipe is easily doubled or halved.

INGREDIENT	VOLUME (U.S.)	WEIGHT (U.S.)	WEIGHT (METRIC)
Lukewarm water	1 cup	8 ounces	225 grams
Whole wheat flour	2 cups	10 ounces	285 grams
Kosher salt[1]	1–1½ teaspoons	—	—
Oil	2 tablespoons	1 ounce	30 grams

[1]Can decrease to taste (see page 20).

Visit PizzaIn5.com, where you'll find recipes, photos, videos, and instructional material. See page 53 for outdoor grill instructions.

1. **Mixing and storing the dough:** Mix the flour, salt, oil, and water in a 2-quart bowl, or a lidded (not airtight) food container, without kneading, using a spoon, a food processor (with dough attachment), or a heavy-duty stand mixer (with paddle). If you're not using a machine, you may need to use wet hands to incorporate the last bit of flour.

2. The dough can be used immediately after mixing, though it may be easier to handle after sitting for 30 minutes or more. Refrigerate it in a lidded container and use over the next 5 days.

3. **Preheat a cast-iron skillet over medium heat** until water droplets skitter across the surface and evaporate quickly. Dust the surface of the refrigerated dough with flour and cut off a 2-ounce (golf ball–size) piece. Dust with more flour and quickly shape it into a ball by stretching the surface of the dough around to the bottom on all four sides, rotating the ball a quarter-turn as you go.

4. **Roll out and stretch the dough:** Flatten a piece of the dough with your hands and a rolling pin on a work surface to produce a $1/16$-inch-thick round. Dust with flour to keep the dough from adhering to the surface. Use a dough scraper to unstick the dough as needed.

5. Carefully lift the dough and lay it onto the hot pan. Allow it to cook for about 30 seconds, then turn to cook the other side for another 30 seconds. Once the dough is set, turn on another burner to medium-high heat and lay the dough directly over the

flame, using a pair of metal tongs. Turn the dough with the tongs until it has puffed; remove from heat. Repeat with remaining dough.

If you omit the stage of cooking these doughs over a live flame you will have supple flat breads that can be used as soft tortillas, which can be used as wraps or soft tacos.

Roti or Flour Tortilla (Non-Yeasted Dough)

"My husband's family is from Trinidad and whenever we all get together for a special occasion we make roti and several pots of curry. It is always a joyful frenzy of conversation and eating too much."—Zoë

This dough is very similar to chapati dough, but made with all-purpose flour. It is excellent for dipping into curry or filling like a burrito.

Makes about six 6-inch roti or tortillas. This recipe is easily doubled or halved.

INGREDIENT	VOLUME (U.S.)	WEIGHT (U.S.)	WEIGHT (METRIC)
Lukewarm water	¾ cup	6 ounces	170 grams
Kosher salt[1]	1-1½ teaspoons	—	—
Oil	2 tablespoons	1 ounce	30 grams
Unbleached all-purpose flour	2 cups	10 ounces	280 grams
Extra flour for rolling dough.			

[1]Can decrease to taste (see page 20).

Follow the directions for mixing and cooking chapati, pages 100–101.

Corn Tortilla (Non-Yeasted and Gluten-Free Corn Dough)

This dough is made with pure masa flour, so it is gluten-free and has a lovely corn flavor. We roll it out thin, cook it in a skillet, and then toast the flatbreads over an open flame on the stove.

Makes about six 6-inch tortillas. This recipe is easily doubled or halved.

INGREDIENT	VOLUME (U.S.)	WEIGHT (U.S.)	WEIGHT (METRIC)
Lukewarm water	1¾ cups	14 ounces	400 grams
Kosher salt[1]	1–1½ teaspoons	—	—
Oil	2 tablespoons	1 ounce	30 grams
Masa harina (corn flour)	2 cups	8 ounces	230 grams
Extra flour for rolling dough.			

[1]Can decrease to taste (see page 20).

1. **Mixing and storing the dough:** Mix the flour, salt, oil, and water in a 2-quart bowl, or a lidded (not airtight) food container, without kneading, using a spoon, a food processor (with dough attachment), or a heavy-duty stand mixer (with paddle). If you're not using a machine, you may need to use wet hands to incorporate the last bit of flour.

2. The dough can be used immediately after mixing, though it may be easier to handle after sitting for 30 minutes or more. Refrigerate it in a lidded container and use over the next 5 days.

Visit PizzaIn5.com, where you'll find recipes, photos, videos, and instructional material. See page 53 for outdoor grill instructions.

NO-FAIL GLUTEN-FREE ROLL-OUT: If you are having trouble rolling out the dough using rice flour, here's a no-fail trick. You can roll it out between a sheet of parchment paper (or a nonstick silicone mat) and plastic wrap. Just sprinkle the parchment with rice flour, place the dough on it, sprinkle the dough with more flour, and place a piece of plastic wrap over the top. Roll with your pin to the desired thickness. Check once in a while to make sure the dough is not sticking to the plastic wrap. If it is, just gently lift it up and sprinkle the dough with more flour. Once the dough is the right thickness, cover with your toppings and slide the pizza into the oven right on the parchment paper or nonstick silicone mat.

3. **Preheat a cast-iron griddle** over medium-high heat, until a drop of water skitters across the surface and evaporates quickly.

4. **Roll out the dough** by breaking off a 2-ounce (golf ball–size) piece of dough; it will not have any stretchiness like wheat doughs. Roll out the dough directly on a pizza peel covered generously with corn flour. Sprinkle the surface of the dough with more corn flour and cover the dough with plastic wrap. Roll to a ⅛-inch-thick round. As you are rolling out the dough, use a dough scraper to make sure that the dough isn't sticking to the peel; add more flour if needed. Gently pull off the plastic.

5. Carefully slide the dough onto the hot griddle. Allow it to cook for about 30 seconds, and then turn with a spatula to cook the other side for another 30 seconds. Once the dough is set, turn on another burner to medium-high heat and lay the dough directly over the flame using a pair of metal tongs. Turn the dough with the tongs until it has charred slightly, and then remove it from the heat. Repeat with remaining dough.

Injera: Ethiopian Flatbread

This traditional Ethiopian flatbread is yeasted dough made with teff flour, which resembles a pancake batter more than a bread dough. It is cooked in a pan on the stove like a crepe. The distinctive sour flavor comes from a long fermentation. Some recipes call for adding a sour starter, but we got the idea for substituting beer from Zoë's family friend, Tefera Landis, who is from Ethiopia. His method jump-starts all the flavor, without having to wait for a long fermentation.

Makes about twelve 6-inch flatbreads

INGREDIENT	VOLUME (U.S.)	WEIGHT (U.S.)	WEIGHT (METRIC)
Beer	1 cup	8 ounces	225 grams
Lukewarm water	1 cup	8 ounces	225
Granulated yeast[1]	2 teaspoons	—	—
Kosher salt[1]	1-1½ teaspoons	—	—
Teff flour	1 cup	5¼ ounces	150 grams
Unbleached all-purpose flour	1 cup	5 ounces	140 grams

[1]Can decrease to taste (see pages 18 and 20).

1. **Mixing and storing the dough:** Mix the yeast and salt with the beer and water in a 2-quart bowl, or a lidded (not airtight) food container.

2. Mix in the remaining dry ingredients, using a spoon. The dough is more like a batter so it will be very loose.

Visit PizzaIn5.com, where you'll find recipes, photos, videos, and instructional material. See page 53 for outdoor grill instructions.

3. Cover (not airtight), and allow it to rest at room temperature until the dough rises and collapses, approximately 2 hours.

4. The dough can be used immediately after its initial rise, though its distinct sour flavor will be more developed in 3 to 5 days. The longer you let it sit, the stronger the flavor. Refrigerate it in a lidded (not airtight) container and use over the next 14 days.

5. **Cook the *injera* in a well-seasoned crepe pan or nonstick skillet.** Coat the surface with oil and heat to medium. Pour a thin layer of the *injera* dough in the pan and swirl it around to coat. It will look like a thick crepe. Once the top of the dough is set, about 2 minutes, carefully flip it and cook on the other side for another minute.

6. Serve with dips and stews.

VARIATION: Gluten-Free *Injera*

INGREDIENT	VOLUME (U.S.)	WEIGHT (U.S.)	WEIGHT (METRIC)
Lukewarm water	2 cups	16 ounces	455 grams
Granulated yeast[1]	2 teaspoons	—	—
Kosher salt[1]	1-1/2 teaspoons	—	—
Teff flour	2 cups	10 1/2 ounces	300 grams

[1]Can decrease to taste (see pages 18 and 20).

Savory Brioche

Traditional brioche is sweetened with a bit of sugar or honey and is used in savory recipes as well as desserts. For this book we decided to go to extremes: a dough that is sweet (see page 254) for our dessert pizzas and this version, with no sugar at all, for the savory pies. They are both rich and flavorful, but in two distinct ways.

Makes enough dough for at least eight ½-pound pizzas or flatbreads (about 12 inches across). The recipe is easily doubled or halved.

INGREDIENT	VOLUME (U.S.)	WEIGHT (U.S.)	WEIGHT (METRIC)
Lukewarm water	1½ cups	12 ounces	340 grams
Granulated yeast[1]	1 tablespoon	0.35 ounce	10 grams
Kosher salt[1]	1–1½ tablespoons	0.63–0.94 ounce	17–25 grams
Large eggs, lightly beaten	6	12 ounce	350 grams
Unbleached all-purpose flour	6½ cups	2 pounds	900 grams
Unsalted butter, melted and slightly cooled	1 cup (2 sticks)	8 ounces	230 grams

[1]Can decrease to taste (see pages 18 and 20).

1. **Mixing and storing the dough:** Mix the yeast, salt, and eggs with the water in a 5-quart bowl, or a lidded (not airtight) food container.

2. Mix in the flour and butter without kneading, using a spoon, a 14-cup capacity food processor (with dough attachment), or a heavy-duty stand mixer (with paddle). If you're not using a machine, you may need to use wet hands to incorporate the last bit of flour.

3. Cover (not airtight), and allow it to rest at room temperature until the dough rises and collapses (or flattens on top), approximately 2 hours.

4. The dough will be loose, but will firm up when chilled. Don't try to use it without chilling for at least 3 hours or until firm. Refrigerate it in a lidded (not airtight) container and use over the next 5 days. Or store the dough for up to 3 weeks in the freezer in ½-pound portions. When using frozen dough, thaw it in the refrigerator overnight before use.

5. **On pizza or flatbread day,** roll out or stretch the dough into a thin round and finish with your favorite toppings, using many of the recipes in this book.

Tomato Toppings

The key to great pizza with tomato is having the best ingredients you can get your hands on. We use tomatoes straight from the can, sliced fresh from the garden, or made into a sauce. Garden-fresh tomatoes sliced right onto a pizza are glorious, but for most of us, the canned variety is more convenient and available twelve months a year.

We usually use canned Italian-style plum tomatoes, and often put them right onto pizza uncooked, without any preparation at all. They are sold:

- **Whole or diced:** These need to be strained and pressed (or reduced) of excess liquid (measure after straining/pressing/reducing). Use a food processor or a knife to produce a smooth or chunky result to your liking.
- **Crushed or pureed:** These usually require no reduction or other pre-treatment, unless they're very thin and watery. Products labeled as tomato sauce also work, and likewise don't require straining, pressing, or reducing.

MAKING SAUCES FROM CANNED OR FRESH TOMATO

If the uncooked plain canned tomatoes are too austere for your taste, add garlic, herbs and even capers to create a sauce with more complex flavors. You can mix garden-fresh tomatoes with herbs and puree (or simply chop) all the raw ingredients together. This produces a delicate, clean, and bright flavor. Cooking it all together and reducing it will give you a smoother, richer, sweeter, and thicker sauce, more in the American style.

Visit PizzaIn5.com, where you'll find recipes, photos, videos, and instructional material. See page 53 for outdoor grill instructions.

Makes about 4 cups of sauce from canned tomato. The recipe is easily doubled or halved.

Four 14½-ounce or two 28-ounce cans crushed or diced tomatoes: the world's simplest pizza topping

Any or all of the following can be added to the sauce to create a more complex flavor.

One 6-ounce can tomato paste (optional, for a sweeter, thicker effect)
2 garlic cloves, minced (optional)
1½ teaspoons dried oregano or 1 tablespoon fresh (optional)
1 teaspoon chopped fresh basil (optional)
2 teaspoons capers (optional)
¼ teaspoon hot red pepper flakes (optional)
Anchovies to taste (optional)
Salt and freshly ground black pepper to taste

1. Put all the ingredients in a large saucepan and simmer uncovered over medium-low heat until sauce thickens to your taste. (**Reduce the sauce until it's very thick** for the Chicago-style pizza on page 191.) Use a food processor or an immersion blender to make the sauce as smooth or as chunky as you like.

2. Refrigerate for up to 5 days or freeze.

VARIATION: Superfast Raw (Small Volume)
Run through a food processer until smooth: one 14½-ounce can of tomatoes and one 6-ounce can of tomato paste. Makes enough sauce

Master Recipe, Pizza Margherita, page 59

Master Recipe, Pizza Margherita, page 59

Fresh Cherry Tomato Pizza, page 121

Barbecued Chicken Pizza, page 124

Curried Sweet Potato, Lentil, and Arugula Pizza, page 129

Brussels Sprouts, Smoked Pancetta, and Pecorino Pizza, page 131

Rainbow Beet Pizza, page 135

White Clam Pizza, page 144

Hawaiian Pizza (Pineapple, Ham, and Macadamia Nuts), page 152

Individual Breakfast Pizzas, page 159

Provençal Onion Tart with Cracked Egg and Anchovy, page 165

Stovetop Pizza, page 170

Thick-Crusted Sicilian-Style Pizza with Onions, page 173

Thick-Crusted Roman Eggplant Pizza, page 176

Roman-Style Sandwiches, page 176

for several pizzas and doesn't need any draining or reduction of liquid to create a thick sauce. You can add any of the optional ingredients; let the mixture sit for two hours to allow the flavors to marry if you have time.

Visit PizzaIn5.com, where you'll find recipes, photos, videos, and instructional material. See page 53 for outdoor grill instructions.

Bolognese (Meat) Sauce

This is a fast sauce that is chock-full of meaty flavor, made richer by adding a bit of milk and cheese. Use it on any of the doughs to create a hearty pizza.

Makes about 5 cups sauce. The recipe is easily doubled or halved.

2 tablespoons olive oil
1 small white onion, finely chopped
1 carrot, grated
1 celery stalk, finely chopped
2 garlic cloves, minced
1 pound ground meat (beef, pork, and/or lamb)
1 teaspoon chopped fresh oregano (or $1/2$ teaspoon dried oregano)
1 teaspoon chopped fresh thyme (or $1/2$ teaspoon dried thyme)
1 teaspoon salt
2 tablespoons tomato paste
$1/3$ cup whole milk
One 14-ounce can diced or crushed tomatoes

1. In a large skillet, sauté the onions, carrot, celery, and garlic in the olive oil over medium-low heat, just until soft, about 5 minutes. Add the meat, turn the heat up to medium-high, and cook until browned, breaking the meat up as it cooks. Add the herbs, salt, tomato paste, milk, and tomatoes.

2. Simmer for 20 to 30 minutes, depending on how thick you like your sauce, stirring occasionally.

3. Refrigerate for up to 5 days or freeze for later use.

Homemade Barbecue Sauce

We developed this recipe for the Barbecued Chicken Pizza (page 124), but it's also great on ordinary cheese pizzas—it's a real change of pace. Once you start making your own barbecue sauce, it will be hard to go back to the jarred stuff.

Makes 3 cups sauce

1 tablespoon neutral-flavored vegetable oil or olive oil
1 onion, finely chopped
One 28-ounce can diced or pureed tomatoes
1 cup ketchup
2/3 cup white vinegar
1/4 cup orange juice
1/4 cup dark brown sugar, firmly packed
1 tablespoon chili powder
1 tablespoon paprika
2 teaspoons kosher salt
1 teaspoon freshly ground black pepper, or more to taste

1. In a skillet, sauté the onions in the oil until lightly browned. Add the remaining ingredients and bring to a simmer. Cook for 15 minutes over low to medium heat.

2. Run the sauce through the food processor (or use an immersion blender) if you used diced tomatoes and you prefer a smooth sauce.

3. Refrigerate for up to 7 days or freeze for later use.

Visit PizzaIn5.com, where you'll find recipes, photos, videos, and instructional material. See page 53 for outdoor grill instructions.

ROASTING GARLIC: Wrap the unpeeled garlic cloves in aluminum foil and bake for 45 minutes at 400°F. Allow to cool, and cut off the tops of the heads. Squeeze out the roasted garlic and set aside.

Pesto: Basil or Greens, from Farm to Table

Pesto is the classic garlicky green sauce of northern Italy, and it's delicious on pizza. Use pesto in place of tomato sauce for the simplest pesto pizza, or combine it with savory meats to produce a whole meal in a pizza—*soppressata* is one of our favorite pairings (see page 127). Traditional basil pesto is a great place to start, but we enjoy experimenting with more offbeat greens (see Variation on page 115). Because traditional pesto is made with cheese, you can try using it without any additional cheese topping, or omit the cheese from the recipe for a purer basil flavor. Likewise, you can omit the nuts for a simpler, less-rich sauce. For a less pungent effect, roast the garlic before use (see sidebar).

Basil or greens can also be used in plain olive oil–based vegetable sauces, without nuts *or* cheese. When topped with mozzarella or other rich cheese, you'll hardly notice the difference (see Variation on page 116).

"One summer my family bought a CSA (community-supported agriculture) share, and week after week, a bounty of wonderful cooking greens arrived: collards, kale, kohlrabi, chard, beet greens, and my favorite, broccoli rabe. My kids quickly grew tired of eating them as vegetable side dishes so we used them as fantastic, nutritious, and economical substitutes for basil in pesto (see Variation on page 115)."—Jeff

Makes 1¹/₂ cups pesto

4 garlic cloves, raw or roasted (see sidebar, page 114)

2 cups fresh basil, loosely packed

¹/₂ cup pine nuts (can substitute walnuts, almonds, or other nuts)

2 ounces grated Parmigiano-Reggiano cheese

1 cup olive oil

¹/₂ teaspoon kosher salt

¹/₄ teaspoon freshly ground black pepper

1. Process all ingredients in a food processor until smooth.

2. Refrigerator for up to 7 days or freeze for later use.

VARIATION: Pesto with Spinach, Broccoli Rabe, Kohlrabi Greens, Beet Greens, Collards, or Kale

Chop a full bunch of greens and sauté them in ¹/₄ cup of olive oil until tender. Unless you're looking for lots of crunch (Jeff's choice), the tougher greens (collards or kale) can benefit from a little braising; add ¹/₄ cup water after a brief sauté and simmer, covered, for 15 minutes (don't do this with spinach, in fact, be sure to cook off excess water if you're using it). Allow to cool and run through the food processor until smooth. Substitute for basil in the recipe above, decreasing olive oil to ³/₄ cup.

For a very simple and light green sauce that also works well on pizza, you can omit the nuts and cheese; decrease the oil to ¹/₂ cup.

VARIATION: Pesto and Tomato Pizza

Put alternating patches of pesto and crushed tomato on your dough, interspersing with your favorite pizza cheese. This works beautifully with soft or firm cheeses (see the color photo, back cover).

Béchamel: Sauce for "White" Pizzas

What pizza joints call "white sauce" is related to what the French call "béchamel" (*báysh-ah-mel*), so here's a very simple version that works every time—loosely based on Julia Child's in *Mastering the Art of French Cooking*. Though Julia would be scandalized, you don't absolutely have to simmer the milk before you add it to the pan, though you'll have to be a little more vigorous with your whisking to prevent lumps. The whole milk and butter version is the most flavorful and soul-satisfying, but the recipe works with skim milk and oil.

"In high school I worked in the kind of Italian place where everything, pizza or not, came with tomato and cheese. By the 1980s, these typical East Coast places had started offering a 'white' pizza alternative (see page 139), which was code for 'no tomato.' They'd jazz it up with parsley or basil and call it 'green' pizza (see variations on page 115 and 116), spinach pizza (page 139), or at its most expressive, white pizza with clams (page 144)."—Jeff

WHY A NONREACTIVE PAN FOR BÉCHAMEL? When cast-iron is used to make a béchamel, the sauce turns slightly gray. If you prefer your white sauces truly white, use stainless steel.

Makes 2 cups sauce

1^1/$_2$ cups whole or skim milk
2^1/$_2$ tablespoons butter, olive oil, or neutral-flavored oil
3 tablespoons white flour or white rice flour
^{1}/$_4$ teaspoon salt

Visit PizzaIn5.com, where you'll find recipes, photos, videos, and instructional material. See page 53 for outdoor grill instructions.

1. Bring the milk to a slow simmer in a small saucepan or in the microwave. Meanwhile, melt the butter or oil in a nonreactive saucepan or skillet over medium-low heat, then add the flour. Continue whisking, allowing the flour-butter mixture to simmer but not to brown.

2. Slowly add the hot milk to the flour-butter mixture, blending constantly with the whisk, and simmer until it thickens nicely, usually 1 to 3 minutes. Add the salt, taste, and adjust as needed.

3. Refrigerate for up to 5 days.

VARIATION: Béchamel with Fresh Herbs
In the last minute of simmering, add 2 tablespoons of chopped fresh herbs, such as parsley or basil. If using dried herbs, cut the amounts in half.

VARIATION: Béchamel with Grated Cheese (Alfredo Sauce)
Just as you remove the béchamel from the heat, stir in ¹⁄₂ cup of grated Parmigiano-Reggiano or other hard grating cheese. Makes a terrific base for a wide variety of vegetable or meat pizzas, with or without tomato.

Tomatillo Sauce

Fresh tart tomatillo sauce is a snap to make at home, and goes beautifully with corn-based doughs made into flatbreads or bread sticks (pages 229 and 92) for Southwestern and Mexican-inspired hors d'oeuvres. It's great as a simple sauce, or try the more complex-flavored *salsa verde* variation below.

Makes 2 cups sauce

1 pound tomatillos (about 10), or one 14-ounce can whole tomatillos (discard liquid in the can)

$1/4$ cup water

1 teaspoon sugar

$1/4$ teaspoon kosher salt

1. Peel the papery skin off the tomatillos and rinse them. Place them in a saucepan, add the water, sugar, and salt, then simmer, covered, over low heat until soft, about 15 minutes. Add a tablespoon or so of water if they seem to be drying out.

2. Simmer until thickened; canned tomatillos usually require more reduction than fresh.

3. Cool the tomatillos, then run through the food processor.

VARIATION: *Salsa Verde*
Leftover tomatillo sauce can be used as the base for a wonderful **salsa verde** (green sauce): Just add 2 tablespoons of minced cilantro, 2 tablespoons of

chopped onions, and 1 teaspoon of finely minced jalapeño or serrano pepper (seeded and cored). Run through a food processor for a smoother sauce, and consider using protective gloves for the peppers if you are mincing them by hand.

7

THIN-CRUST PIZZAS AND FLATBREADS

Fresh Cherry Tomato Pizza

Use any cherry tomatoes you like, but a mix of colors makes for a gorgeous pie and they really do have a variety of flavors, so try mixing them up. You need to cut the tomatoes in half, even if they are tiny, so they won't explode in the oven.

"One summer the only tomatoes my garden produced were the tiniest cherry tomatoes, both yellow and red. They were little, but they packed intense flavor and sang on top of a pizza with the basil that grew next to them."—Zoë

Makes one 12-inch pizza

$^{1}/_{2}$ pound (orange-size portion) lean or gluten-free dough from pages 59–98

12 cherry tomatoes (more if you have tiny ones), halved

3 ounces fresh mozzarella or fontina cheese, cut into $^{1}/_{2}$-inch chunks (see page 50)

5 fresh basil leaves

1 tablespoon olive oil

Pinch of coarse salt

Flour, cornmeal, parchment paper, or rice flour for the pizza peel

1. **Prepare and measure** all toppings in advance.

2. **Preheat a baking stone at your oven's highest temperature for at least 30 minutes** (see "Why Such a Short Preheat," page 49). Sprinkle a pizza peel liberally with flour. Dust the surface of the refrigerated dough with flour and cut off a $^{1}/_{2}$-pound (orange-size) piece. Dust with more flour and quickly shape it into a ball by stretching the surface of the dough around to the bottom on all four sides, rotating the ball a quarter-turn as you go.

3. **Stretch the pizza crust:** Flatten the dough with your hands and/or a rolling pin on a work surface, or directly onto a wooden pizza peel, to produce a $^{1}/_{8}$-inch-thick round. Dust with flour to keep the dough from adhering to the surface. Use a dough scraper to unstick the dough as needed, and transfer to a pizza peel if you haven't already stretched the dough on one. (See page 47 if you'd rather bake on a sheet pan.) When you're finished, the dough round should have enough flour under it to move easily when you shake the peel.

4. **Add the toppings:** Scatter the cherry tomatoes haphazardly over the dough, some with their cut side up, some down. Add the cheese and basil, then drizzle with olive oil and sprinkle with a pinch of coarse salt.

5. **Slide the pizza onto the preheated stone** (see Step 11, page 67): If you're using a sheet pan, place it right on the stone. Check for doneness in 8 to 10 minutes, and turn the pizza around in the oven if one side is browning faster than the other.

6. Allow to cool slightly, preferably on a wire cooling rack. Cut into wedges and serve.

VARIATION: With Red Cabbage

Sauté a small onion in $1/8$ cup olive oil in a roomy skillet until it begins to brown. Thinly slice a quarter-head of a small red cabbage and add, continuing to sauté until cabbage is wilted. Add salt and pepper to taste, and distribute sparsely between tomatoes in the cheese pizza above (you may not need all of what you prepared). Bake as usual.

Visit PizzaIn5.com, where you'll find recipes, photos, videos, and instructional material. See page 53 for outdoor grill instructions.

Barbecued Chicken Pizza

Barbecue sauce on pizza seems sacrilegious to some, but it's as popular as it is for a good reason: the peppery, vinegary barbecue sauce is nicely balanced by the rich cheese. Homemade sauce (page 113) is phenomenal, but you can use jarred versions as well. Serve with homemade coleslaw (page 126) or another crunchy and refreshing salad. If you like your pizza hot and spicy, use the optional *pepperoncini* (hot Italian peppers widely available in jars).

Makes one 12-inch pizza

2 boneless skinless chicken thighs, brushed with olive oil and seasoned with salt and freshly ground black pepper

$1/2$ pound (orange-size portion) lean or gluten-free dough from pages 59–98

$1/3$ cup barbecue sauce, homemade (page 113) or jarred

3 ounces gouda or other medium-soft cheese (see page 10) cut into $1/2$-inch chunks

$1/2$ small red onion, sliced very thinly

2 *pepperoncini*, thinly sliced and seeded (optional)

1 teaspoon chopped fresh cilantro (optional)

Flour, cornmeal, parchment paper, or rice flour for the pizza peel

1. **Prepare and measure** all toppings in advance.

2. Grill the chicken over medium heat on a grill, until barely cooked through. Cool briefly, then chop coarsely into bite-size chunks.

3. **Preheat a baking stone at your oven's highest temperature for at least 30 minutes** (see "Why Such a Short Preheat," page 49). Sprinkle a pizza peel liberally with flour. Dust the surface of the refrigerated dough with flour and cut off a ½-pound (orange-size) piece. Dust with more flour and quickly shape it into a ball by stretching the surface of the dough around to the bottom on all four sides, rotating the ball a quarter-turn as you go.

4. **Stretch the pizza crust:** Flatten the dough with your hands and/or a rolling pin on a work surface, or directly onto a wooden pizza peel, to produce a ⅛-inch-thick round. Dust with flour to keep the dough from adhering to the surface. Use a dough scraper to unstick the dough as needed, and transfer to a pizza peel if you haven't already stretched the dough on one. (See page 47 if you'd rather bake on a sheet pan.) When you're finished, the dough round should have enough flour under it to move easily when you shake the peel.

5. **Add the toppings:** Spread the barbecue sauce over the dough, then top with chicken, cheese, onion, and *pepperoncini*, if using.

6. **Slide the pizza onto the preheated stone** (see Step 11, page 67): If you're using a sheet pan, place it right on the stone. Check for doneness in 8 to 10 minutes, and turn the pizza around in the oven if one side is browning faster than the other.

7. Sprinkle with cilantro, if desired, and allow to cool slightly, preferably on a wire cooling rack. Cut into wedges and serve with coleslaw (page 126).

Visit PizzaIn5.com, where you'll find recipes, photos, videos, and instructional material. See page 53 for outdoor grill instructions.

Homemade Coleslaw

Makes about 5 cups

1 head green cabbage (about 2 pounds), sliced thin
2 scallions, sliced, or a bunch of chives, snipped
2 carrots, peeled and grated
3/4 cup sugar
3/4 cup white vinegar
3/4 cup neutral-flavored vegetable oil
1 tablespoon kosher salt
1 teaspoon prepared mustard

1. Toss all the ingredients together in a large bowl and allow to marinate in the refrigerator for about 2 hours, stirring occasionally.

2. Store in the refrigerator for up to 7 days (do not freeze).

Pizza with Soppressata and Piave (or Pepperoni and Mozzarella)

Soppressata, imported from Italy, is probably the model for pepperoni, a sausage style found mainly in America. Rich, spicy, and fabulous, it has become a favored ingredient for American *pizzaioli*. If you can't find it, pepperoni works nicely too. Both are well complemented by the flavor of *Piave*, a firm Italian cheese, or go with your favorite mozzarella.

Makes one 12-inch pizza

^{1}/$_2$ pound (orange-size portion) lean or gluten-free dough from pages 59–98

^{1}/$_3$ cup tomato toppings (see page 109)

3 ounces *Piave* or other medium-firm cheese (see page 13), cut into ^{1}/$_2$-inch chunks (see page 50)

3 ounces thinly sliced *soppressata* or pepperoni, rendered of some of its fat in the microwave or a frying pan

Flour, cornmeal, parchment paper, or rice flour for the pizza peel

1. **Prepare and measure** all toppings in advance.

2. **Preheat a baking stone at your oven's highest temperature for at least 30 minutes** (see "Why Such a Short Preheat," page 49). Sprinkle a pizza peel liberally with flour. Dust the surface of the refrigerated dough with flour and cut off a ^{1}/$_2$-pound (orange-size) piece. Dust with more flour and quickly shape it into a ball by stretching the surface of the dough around to the bottom on all four sides, rotating the ball a quarter-turn as you go.

Visit PizzaIn5.com, where you'll find recipes, photos, videos, and instructional material. See page 53 for outdoor grill instructions.

3. **Stretch the pizza crust:** Flatten the dough with your hands and/or a rolling pin on a work surface, or directly onto a wooden pizza peel, to produce a 1/8-inch-thick round. Dust with flour to keep the dough from adhering to the surface. Use a dough scraper to unstick the dough as needed, and transfer to a pizza peel if you haven't already stretched the dough on one. (See page 47 if you'd rather bake on a sheet pan.) When you're finished, the dough round should have enough flour under it to move easily when you shake the peel.

4. **Add the toppings:** Spread the tomato over the dough, add the cheese, and finish with the meat.

5. **Slide the pizza onto the preheated stone** (see Step 11, page 67): If you're using a sheet pan, place it right on the stone. Check for doneness in 8 to 10 minutes, and turn the pizza around in the oven if one side is browning faster than the other.

6. Allow to cool slightly, preferably on a wire cooling rack. Cut into wedges and serve.

Curried Sweet Potato, Lentil, and Arugula Pizza

We're big believers in dropping dressed, raw greens onto hot pizza—you end up with a complete and delicious meal in a wedge. It works with ordinary tomato and mozzarella pies, but here we decided to improvise in the middle of a photo shoot. If you don't have any of the Brenda Langton's Curried Lentil Soup (see page 227), pureed cooked butternut squash works well (see sidebar).

Makes one 12-inch pizza

$^1/_2$ pound (orange-size portion) lean or gluten-free dough from pages 59–98

$^1/_3$ cup Brenda Langton's Curried Lentil Soup (page 227, or see sidebar)

3 ounces mozzarella or other medium-soft cheese, cut into $^1/_2$-inch chunks (see page 10)

Generous handful of raw arugula, lightly dressed with olive oil just before serving

Flour, cornmeal, parchment paper, or rice flour for the pizza peel

1. **Prepare and measure** all toppings in advance.

2. **Preheat a baking stone at your oven's highest temperature for at**

∾

BUTTERNUT OR OTHER WINTER SQUASH IS A DELICIOUS SWAP FOR THE SWEET POTATO LENTIL SOUP ON THIS PIZZA: Cut the squash in half and roast in the oven, cut-side down, on an oiled baking sheet at 400°F for 30 to 45 minutes or until soft. Scrape the squash from the shell, and puree with two cloves garlic, 1 teaspoon curry powder, and 2 tablespoons olive oil or water (may need more to reach the consistency of a spreadable sauce). Generously season with salt and pepper to taste.

Visit PizzaIn5.com, where you'll find recipes, photos, videos, and instructional material. See page 53 for outdoor grill instructions.

least 30 minutes (see "Why Such a Short Preheat," page 49). Sprinkle a pizza peel liberally with flour. Dust the surface of the refrigerated dough with flour and cut off a ½-pound (orange-size) piece. Dust with more flour and quickly shape it into a ball by stretching the surface of the dough around to the bottom on all four sides, rotating the ball a quarter-turn as you go.

3. **Stretch the pizza crust:** Flatten the dough with your hands and/or a rolling pin on a work surface, or directly onto a wooden pizza peel, to produce a ⅛-inch-thick round. Dust with flour to keep the dough from adhering to the surface. Use a dough scraper to unstick the dough as needed, and transfer to a pizza peel if you haven't already stretched the dough on one. (See page 47 if you'd rather bake on a sheet pan.) When you're finished, the dough round should have enough flour under it to move easily when you shake the peel.

4. **Add the toppings:** Spread the soup or squash over the dough, then distribute the cheese.

5. **Slide the pizza onto the preheated stone** (see Step 11, page 67): If you're using a sheet pan, place it right on the stone. Check for doneness in 8 to 10 minutes and turn the pizza around in the oven if one side is browning faster than the other.

6. Top with arugula immediately after removing the pizza from the oven.

7. Allow to cool slightly, preferably on a wire cooling rack. Cut into wedges and serve.

Brussels Sprouts, Smoked Pancetta, and Pecorino Pizza

This pizza is a terrific illustration of how the hard Italian cheese known as pecorino Romano can perk up the flavor of mild toppings on pizza—the result is an explosion of flavor. Mushroom lovers can swap $1/2$ cup raw or sautéed thinly sliced mushrooms for the Brussels sprouts.

Makes one 12-inch pizza

$1/2$ pound (orange-size portion) lean or gluten-free dough from pages 59–98

$1/3$ cup Béchamel Sauce (page 117)

3 ounces aged, smoked, or regular gouda cheese, cut into $1/2$-inch chunks (see page 50)

4 small Brussels sprouts, steamed lightly and cut into $1/8$-inch-thick slices

1 to 2 ounces smoked pancetta, cut into 1-inch squares

4 very thin slices red onion (use a very sharp thin knife, or preferably a man-doline, see page 136)

2 tablespoons coarsely grated pecorino Romano cheese

Flour, cornmeal, parchment paper, or rice flour for the pizza peel

BRUSSELS SPROUTS SHORTCUT: If you can get the Brussels sprouts sliced really, really thin, on a mandoline or with a very sharp knife, you can skip the steaming step and use them raw.

Visit PizzaIn5.com, where you'll find recipes, photos, videos, and instructional material. See page 53 for outdoor grill instructions.

1. **Prepare and measure** all toppings in advance.

2. **Preheat a baking stone at your oven's highest temperature for at least 30 minutes** (see "Why Such a Short Preheat," page 49). Sprinkle a pizza peel liberally with flour. Dust the surface of the refrigerated dough with flour and cut off a $1/2$-pound (orange-size) piece. Dust with more flour and quickly shape it into a ball by stretching the surface of the dough around to the bottom on all four sides, rotating the ball a quarter-turn as you go.

3. **Stretch the pizza crust:** Flatten the dough with your hands and/or a rolling pin on a work surface, or directly onto a wooden pizza peel, to produce a $1/8$-inch-thick round. Dust with flour to keep the dough from adhering to the surface. Use a dough scraper to unstick the dough as needed, and transfer to a pizza peel if you haven't already stretched the dough on one. (See page 47 if you'd rather bake on a sheet pan.) When you're finished, the dough round should have enough flour under it to move easily when you shake the peel.

4. **Add the toppings:** Spread the sauce over the dough, then distribute the gouda cheese, Brussels sprouts, pancetta, and onions. Finish with the pecorino Romano.

5. **Slide the pizza onto the preheated stone** (see Step 11, page 67): If you're using a sheet pan, place it right on the stone. Check for doneness in 8 to 10 minutes, and turn the pizza around in the oven if one side is browning faster than the other.

6. Allow to cool slightly, preferably on a wire cooling rack. Cut into wedges and serve.

Thin-Crusted Zucchini Pie (Flowers Optional)

"The first time I ate pizza with zucchini flowers was in Rome. It was summer and every menu included these seasonal beauties in some form. The flesh of the zucchini was sliced incredibly thin and the blossoms were tossed on just before hitting the hot oven. With nothing but olive oil and salt and pepper as seasoning, this pizza is wonderful, but add a thin layer of pesto and it really sings."—Zoë

Makes one 12-inch pizza

1/4 pound (peach-size portion) lean or gluten-free dough from pages 59–98

3 tablespoons pesto (page 114)

2 zucchinis, sliced into very thin coins (see mandoline sidebar, page 136)

3 ounces soft goat cheese *(chèvre)*

2 zucchini blossoms (optional)

2 tablespoons olive oil

Salt and freshly ground black pepper to taste

Flour, cornmeal, parchment paper, or rice flour for the pizza peel

1. **Prepare and measure** all toppings in advance.

2. **Preheat a baking stone at your oven's highest temperature for at least 30 minutes** (see "Why Such a Short Preheat," page 49). Sprinkle a pizza peel liberally with flour. Dust the surface of the refrigerated dough with flour and cut off a 1/4-pound (peach-size) piece. Dust with more flour and quickly shape it into a ball by stretching the surface of the dough around to the bottom on all four sides, rotating the ball a quarter-turn as you go.

Visit PizzaIn5.com, where you'll find recipes, photos, videos, and instructional material. See page 53 for outdoor grill instructions.

3. **Stretch the pizza crust:** Flatten the dough with your hands and/or a rolling pin on a work surface, or directly onto a wooden pizza peel, to produce a $1/16$-inch-thick round. Dust with flour to keep the dough from adhering to the surface. Use a dough scraper to unstick the dough as needed, and transfer to a pizza peel if you haven't already stretched the dough on one. (See page 47 if you'd rather bake on a sheet pan.) When you're finished, the dough round should have enough flour under it to move easily when you shake the peel.

4. **Add the toppings:** Spread the pesto over the dough, then add the zucchini and cheese. Tear the blossoms, if using, into a few pieces and scatter over the pizza, drizzle with olive oil, and sprinkle with salt and pepper.

5. **Slide the pizza onto the preheated stone** (see Step 11, page 67): If you're using a sheet pan, place it right on the stone. Check for doneness in 8 to 10 minutes and turn the pizza around in the oven if one side is browning faster than the other.

6. Allow to cool slightly, preferably on a wire cooling rack. Cut into wedges and serve.

Rainbow Beet Pizza

You'll want to make this pizza if for no other reason than its gorgeous looks: a shimmering rainbow of colors. The sweetness of the beets is matched by the slight sharpness of the cheese. Add just a little salt and pepper to bring out the flavors, and this pizza is all about the subtle taste of beets. It might even convert the non-beet lovers in your family.

Makes one 12-inch pizza

$1/2$ pound (orange-size portion) lean or gluten-free dough from pages 59–98

4 ounces provolone, cheddar, or other sharp cheese, shredded or thinly sliced

4 small beets (red, orange, and yellow), washed, peeled, sliced very thin (preferably on a mandoline, see page 136)

1 tablespoon olive oil for drizzling

Salt and freshly ground black pepper to taste

Flour, cornmeal, parchment paper, or rice flour for the pizza peel

1. **Prepare and measure** all toppings in advance.

2. **Preheat a baking stone at your oven's highest temperature for at least 30 minutes** (see "Why Such a Short Preheat," page 49). Sprinkle a pizza peel liberally with flour. Dust the surface of the refrigerated dough with flour and cut off a $1/2$-pound (orange-size) piece. Dust with more flour and quickly shape it into a ball by stretching the surface of the dough around to the bottom on all four sides, rotating the ball a quarter-turn as you go.

---

3. **Stretch the pizza crust:** Flatten the dough with your hands and/or a rolling pin on a work surface, or directly onto a wooden pizza peel, to produce a $\frac{1}{8}$-inch-thick round. Dust with flour to keep the dough from adhering to the surface. Use a dough scraper to unstick the dough as needed, and transfer to a pizza peel if you haven't already stretched the dough on one. (See page 47 if you'd rather bake on a sheet pan.) When you're finished, the dough round should have enough flour under it to move easily when you shake the peel.

4. **Add the toppings:** Scatter the cheese over the dough, add the sliced beets in circles, starting from the outside edge and working in to the center, alternating the different colors. Drizzle with olive oil and sprinkle with salt and pepper.

USING A MANDOLINE IS THE EASIEST WAY TO GET THE BEETS PAPER THIN

You can achieve a similar thickness with great patience and a sharp knife. If you are nervous about either of those options, for this recipe you can roast the beets first, which gives them a wonderful sweet flavor and makes them much easier to slice. Just toss them in a 400°F oven for about 40 minutes, peel, and then slice.

5. **Slide the pizza onto the preheated stone** (see Step 11, page 67): If you're using a sheet pan, place it right on the stone. Check for doneness in 8 to 10 minutes and turn the pizza around in the oven if one side is browning faster than the other.

6. Allow to cool slightly, preferably on a wire cooling rack. Cut into wedges and serve.

Roasted Root Vegetable Pizza

The beauty of this recipe is that the vegetables are roasting as the oven pre-heats, to save you precious time and energy. Roasting the vegetables concentrates the natural sugars and intensifies their unique flavors. Toss them with a little balsamic for contrast and then lay the shiny jewels on a bed of creamy ricotta.

Makes one 12-inch pizza

$1/2$ pound (orange-size portion) lean or gluten-free dough from pages 59–98

7 cups $1/4$-inch diced root vegetables (red beets, yellow beets, parsnips, carrots, turnips, or your favorites)

1 cup $1/4$-inch diced fennel bulb (optional)

$1/4$ cup olive oil, plus more for drizzling

$1/4$ cup aged balsamic vinegar

Salt and freshly ground black pepper

$1/2$ cup fresh ricotta cheese

1 garlic clove, finely minced

Flour, cornmeal, parchment paper, or rice flour for the pizza peel

1. **Roast the vegetables:** Toss the root vegetables, fennel bulb, olive oil, vinegar, and salt and pepper together in a large bowl. Lay the mixture evenly over a baking sheet. Turn your oven to its highest setting, as if to preheat for baking the pizza. Place the root vegetables in the cold oven; they will roast as your oven preheats your baking stone. Be sure to turn the vegetables often in the pan to make sure they are not burning, especially on the edges of the pan.

Visit PizzaIn5.com, where you'll find recipes, photos, videos, and instructional material. See page 53 for outdoor grill instructions.

2. When the oven is preheated, the vegetables should be soft. Remove from the oven and set aside. Sprinkle a pizza peel liberally with flour. Dust the surface of the refrigerated dough with flour and cut off a $1/2$-pound (orange-size) piece. Dust with more flour and quickly shape it into a ball by stretching the surface of the dough around to the bottom on all four sides, rotating the ball a quarter-turn as you go.

3. **Stretch the pizza crust:** Flatten the dough with your hands and/or a rolling pin on a work surface, or directly onto a wooden pizza peel, to produce a $1/8$-inch-thick round. Dust with flour to keep the dough from adhering to the surface. Use a dough scraper to unstick the dough as needed, and transfer to a pizza peel if you haven't stretched the dough on one. (See page 47 if you'd rather bake on a sheet pan.) When you're finished, the dough round should have enough flour under it to move easily when you shake the peel.

4. **Add the toppings:** Spread the ricotta and garlic over the dough. Scatter $1^{1}/4$ cups of the root vegetables over the dough (save the rest for another pizza or to toss in a salad), then drizzle with a small amount of olive oil and sprinkle with salt and pepper.

5. **Slide the pizza onto the preheated stone** (see Step 11, page 67): If you're using a sheet pan, place it right on the stone. Check for doneness in 8 to 10 minutes and turn the pizza around in the oven if one side is browning faster than the other.

6. Allow to cool slightly, preferably on a wire cooling rack. Cut into wedges and serve.

White Pizza with Spinach

If you want a break from tomato-based pizza, here's your chance to make one that shines without it.

Makes one 12-inch pizza

$^1/_2$ pound (orange-size portion) lean or gluten-free dough from pages 59–98

$^1/_2$ cup Béchamel Sauce (page 117)

$^1/_3$ cup ricotta cheese

1 generous handful of fresh spinach leaves, chopped and sautéed in 1 tablespoon olive oil until tender

2 ounces mozzarella or other medium-soft cheese, cut into $^1/_2$-inch chunks (see Tips and Techniques, page 50)

Flour, cornmeal, parchment paper, or rice flour for the pizza peel

1. **Prepare and measure** all toppings in advance.

2. **Preheat a baking stone at your oven's highest temperature for at least 30 minutes** (see "Why Such a Short Preheat," page 49). Sprinkle a pizza peel liberally with flour. Dust the surface of the refrigerated dough with flour and cut off a $^1/_2$-pound (orange-size) piece. Dust with more flour and quickly shape it into a ball by stretching the surface of the dough around to the bottom on all four sides, rotating the ball a quarter-turn as you go.

3. **Stretch the pizza crust:** Flatten the dough with your hands and/or a rolling pin on a work surface, or directly onto a wooden pizza peel, to produce a $^1/_8$-inch-thick round. Dust with flour to keep the dough

from adhering to the surface. Use a dough scraper to unstick the dough as needed, and transfer to a pizza peel if you haven't already stretched the dough on one. (See page 47 if you'd rather bake on a sheet pan.) When you're finished, the dough round should have enough flour under it to move easily when you shake the peel.

4. **Add the toppings:** Spread the béchamel over the dough, then dollop with small spoonfuls of ricotta cheese (or use your fingers). The ricotta won't be evenly distributed when you're finished. Scatter the spinach, then intersperse the mozzarella where the ricotta isn't covering well.

5. **Slide the pizza onto the preheated stone** (see Step 11, page 67): If you're using a sheet pan, place it right on the stone. Check for doneness in 8 to 10 minutes and turn the pizza around in the oven if one side is browning faster than the other.

6. Allow to cool slightly, preferably on a wire cooling rack. Cut into wedges and serve with a delicate white wine.

VARIATION: Tofu Pizza

Here's an updated version of your college co-op's attempt at replacing cheese with sliced tofu over tomato sauce. We much prefer tofu as part of a creamy and rich sauce, like béchamel. Prepare the béchamel by putting it through the food processor with 5 ounces of extra-firm tofu; processing until completely smooth. Add more béchamel if the mixture is too thick to spread. Apply to the crust, omit the mozzarella and ricotta, and finish with the sautéed spinach and a tablespoon of finely grated Parmigiano-Reggiano.

Joelein's Winning Chicken Potpie Pizza

We held a contest on our Web site and asked our readers to submit their favorite pizza combination. We collected over 200 tantalizing ideas and had our editors at Thomas Dunne Books help us select the winner. Joelein's concept of a chicken potpie on a pizza made us all hungry and won its place here in the book.

"One day I made a pizza that consisted of a quarter of an onion, leftover corn on the cob, bits of roasted chicken, and dough. With some help from the pantry, the freezer, and my husband, Carlos, chicken potpie pizza was born. It is now a regular meal for our growing family!"—Joelein

Makes one 12-inch pizza

$1/2$ pound (orange-size portion) lean or gluten-free dough from pages 59–98

1 cup Béchamel Sauce (page 117)

4 tablespoons olive oil

$1/4$ cup diced onion

$1/4$ cup carrots in $1/4$-inch dice

$1/4$ cup celery in $1/4$-inch dice

$1/4$ cup Yukon gold potato in $1/4$-inch dice

$1/2$ cup cooked chicken in $1/4$-inch dice

1 garlic clove, minced

$1/4$ cup white button mushrooms in $1/4$-inch dice

$1/4$ cup fresh or frozen peas

$1/4$ cup fresh or frozen corn kernels

$1/2$ teaspoon chopped fresh thyme (or $1/4$ teaspoon dried thyme)

$1/8$ teaspoon ground nutmeg

Salt and freshly ground pepper to taste

Visit PizzaIn5.com, where you'll find recipes, photos, videos, and instructional material. See page 53 for outdoor grill instructions.

2 ounces mozzarella or other medium-soft cheese, cut into $^1/_2$-inch chunks (see Tips and Techniques, page 50)

Flour, cornmeal, parchment paper, or rice flour for the pizza peel

1. **Prepare the toppings:** In a skillet, heat 2 tablespoons of the olive oil over medium heat. Add the onions, carrots, celery, and potatoes and sauté until all the vegetables are just soft. Remove the vegetables from the pan and set aside. Add the remaining 2 tablespoons olive oil to the skillet and sauté the chicken for about 3 minutes. Add the garlic and mushrooms and cook for another minute. Add the cooked vegetables, peas, corn, thyme, nutmeg, salt, and pepper and the béchamel sauce to the chicken and cook for another minute. Set aside.

2. **Preheat a baking stone at your oven's highest temperature for at least 30 minutes** (see "Why Such a Short Preheat," page 49). Sprinkle a pizza peel liberally with flour. Dust the surface of the refrigerated dough with flour and cut off a $^1/_2$-pound (orange-size) piece. Dust with more flour and quickly shape it into a ball by stretching the surface of the dough around to the bottom on all four sides, rotating the ball a quarter-turn as you go.

3. **Stretch the pizza crust:** Flatten the dough with your hands and/or a rolling pin on a work surface, or directly onto a wooden pizza peel, to produce a $^1/_8$-inch-thick round. Dust with flour to keep the dough from adhering to the surface. Use a dough scraper to unstick the dough as needed, and transfer to a pizza peel if you haven't already stretched the dough on one. (See page 47 if you'd rather bake on a sheet pan.) When you're finished, the dough round should have enough flour under it to move easily when you shake the peel.

4. **Add the toppings:** Spread half the potpie filling over the dough, then distribute the cheese. Refrigerate or freeze the remaining topping for another pizza.

5. **Slide the pizza onto the preheated stone** (see Step 11, page 67): If you're using a sheet pan, place it right on the stone. Check for doneness in 8 to 10 minutes and turn the pizza around in the oven if one side is browning faster than the other.

6. Allow to cool slightly, preferably on a wire cooling rack. Cut into wedges and serve.

Visit PizzaIn5.com, where you'll find recipes, photos, videos, and instructional material. See page 53 for outdoor grill instructions.

White Clam Pizza

Béchamel and creamy ricotta cheese make a pillowy bed for succulent briny clams. We use a little Parmigiano-Reggiano on top to enhance browning.

Makes one 12-inch pizza

$^1/_2$ pound (orange-size portion) lean **or** gluten-free dough from pages 59–98
$^1/_2$ cup Béchamel Sauce (page 117)
$^1/_3$ cup ricotta cheese
One 6$^1/_2$-ounce can clam meat, drained
1 tablespoon finely minced flat-leaf parsley
2 tablespoons finely grated Parmigiano-Reggiano cheese
Flour, cornmeal, parchment paper, or rice flour for the pizza peel
Lemon wedges for garnish

1. **Prepare and measure** all toppings in advance.

2. **Preheat a baking stone at your oven's highest temperature for at least 30 minutes** (see "Why Such a Short Preheat," page 49). Sprinkle a pizza peel liberally with flour. Dust the surface of the refrigerated dough with flour and cut off a $^1/_2$-pound (orange-size) piece. Dust with more flour and quickly shape it into a ball by stretching the surface of the dough around to the bottom on all four sides, rotating the ball a quarter-turn as you go.

3. **Stretch the pizza crust:** Flatten the dough with your hands and/or a rolling pin on a work surface, or directly onto a wooden pizza peel, to produce a $^1/_8$-inch-thick round. Dust with flour to keep the

dough from adhering to the surface. Use a dough scraper to unstick the dough as needed, and transfer to a pizza peel if you haven't already stretched the dough on one. (See page 47 if you'd rather bake on a sheet pan.) When you're finished, the dough round should have enough flour under it to move easily when you shake the peel.

4. **Add the toppings:** Spread the béchamel over the dough, then dollop with small spoonfuls of ricotta cheese (or use your fingers). The ricotta won't be evenly distributed when you're finished. Scatter the clams and parsley over the dough, then finish with the Parmigiano.

5. **Slide the pizza onto the preheated stone** (see Step 11, page 67): If you're using a sheet pan, place it right on the stone. Check for doneness in 8 to 10 minutes and turn the pizza around in the oven if one side is browning faster than the other.

6. Allow to cool slightly, preferably on a wire cooling rack. Cut into wedges and serve with lemon wedges for squeezing.

Visit PizzaIn5.com, where you'll find recipes, photos, videos, and instructional material. See page 53 for outdoor grill instructions.

Ancient Greco-Roman Pizza with Feta, Honey, and Sesame Seeds

The ancient Greek author Athenaeus wrote the world's oldest known complete cookbook, *The Deipnosophists*, and it contains what may be civilization's first written pizza recipe, which we adapt here. The ancient Greeks and Romans used spelt flour, not modern wheat, which hadn't been cultivated yet. And they didn't have mozzarella—more likely they used strongly flavored goat cheeses, not unlike today's Greek feta, whose sharpness they mellowed with honey. And there were no tomatoes in Europe until explorers brought them back from the New World in the sixteenth century. Odd to think of Italian food without tomatoes, but there you have it.

Depending on whose translation you believe, "*deipnosophists*" are either "philosophers at dinner," or, according to some experts, "partying professors." Apparently the ancient Greeks made little distinction between "dinner," "feast," and "party," and such gatherings were accompanied by huge clay jugs of wine.

For a terrific variation, try Sue's Goat Cheese Appetizer (page 148) as a super-nutritious topping in place of plain feta.

Makes one 12-inch pizza

$^1/_2$ pound (orange-size portion) spelt dough (page 84; can substitute any lean or
    gluten-free dough from pages 59–98)
4 ounces feta cheese, crumbled
3 tablespoons honey
2 teaspoons sesame seeds
Flour, cornmeal, parchment paper, or rice flour for the pizza peel

1. **Prepare and measure** all toppings in advance.

2. **Preheat a baking stone at your oven's highest temperature for at least
    30 minutes** (see "Why Such a Short Preheat," page 49). Sprinkle a
    pizza peel liberally with flour. Dust the surface of the refrigerated
    dough with flour and cut off a $\frac{1}{2}$-pound (orange-size) piece. Dust
    with more flour and quickly shape it into a ball by stretching the
    surface of the dough around to the bottom on all four sides, rotating
    the ball a quarter-turn as you go.

3. **Stretch the pizza crust:** Flatten the dough with your hands and/or a
    rolling pin on a work surface, or directly onto a wooden pizza peel, to
    produce a $\frac{1}{8}$-inch-thick round. Dust with flour to keep the dough
    from adhering to the surface. Use a dough scraper to unstick the
    dough as needed, and transfer to a pizza peel if you haven't already
    stretched the dough on one. (See page 47 if you'd rather bake on a
    sheet pan.) When you're finished, the dough round should have
    enough flour under it to move easily when you shake the peel.

4. **Add the toppings:** Sprinkle the cheese over the dough, then drizzle
    with honey. Finish with a sprinkling of sesame seeds.

5. **Slide the pizza onto the preheated stone** (see Step 11, page 67): If
    you're using a sheet pan, place it right on the stone. Check for done-
    ness in 8 to 10 minutes and turn the pizza around in the oven if one
    side is browning faster than the other. Feta cheese doesn't flow like
    mozzarella, so don't wait for that to happen.

6. Allow to cool slightly, preferably on a wire cooling rack. Cut into
    wedges and serve.

Visit PizzaIn5.com, where you'll find recipes, photos, videos, and instructional material. See
page 53 for outdoor grill instructions.

Sue's Goat Cheese, Honey, Pumpkin Seed, and Fruit Appetizer

"My friend Sue introduced me to a terrific appetizer based on tangy soft goat cheese (chèvre) softened by fruit, pumpkin seeds, and honey. The more I thought about the flavors, the more it reminded me of our Greco-Roman pizza (page 146). This cheese appetizer is fantastic as a party spread for cut-up flatbread, but if there's any left over, it makes a great pizza topping. Just scoop it up, daub it on the unbaked dough, and follow the baking directions on pages 147. Think of it as a Greco-Roman pizza with 'The Works.'"—Jeff

Makes 6 appetizer portions

1 tablespoon olive oil

2 tablespoons honey or agave syrup

1 teaspoon balsamic vinegar

1 tablespoon water (omit if using agave syrup)

2 pinches of dried oregano

$1/4$ teaspoon salt

1 tablespoon pumpkin seeds (*pepitas*), preferably unsalted (decrease or omit salt if using salted *pepitas*)

1 cup dried fruit (your choice of raisins, golden raisins, chopped apricots, cranberries, chopped dates, chopped figs, or chopped dried mango)

6 ounces soft goat cheese (*chèvre*)

1. Combine all ingredients except cheese in a saucepan and heat gently until heated through and fruit has plumped.

2. Pour over the cheese and serve with flatbread or crackers.

Pear Gorgonzola Pizza with Candied Walnuts

The contrasting flavors of sweet pears and blue cheese are a traditional combination that work beautifully as a pizza that can be served as an appetizer or even for dessert. The salty-sweet walnuts add to the complexity of flavors and give this pizza a crunchy texture.

Makes one 12-inch pizza

1/2 pound (orange-size portion) lean or gluten-free dough from pages 59–98 or Savory Brioche dough (page 107)

2 small, firm pears, cored and thinly sliced (see sidebar, page 150)

2 tablespoons unsalted butter

1/2 teaspoon ground nutmeg

2 ounces Gorgonzola or other blue cheese, crumbled

2 ounces cream cheese

2 tablespoons maple syrup for drizzling

Flour, cornmeal, parchment paper, or rice flour for the pizza peel

Candied Walnuts

1 cup walnut pieces (or your favorite nuts)

2 tablespoons maple syrup

1/4 teaspoon kosher salt

1/4 teaspoon freshly ground black pepper

1. **Prepare the pears:** Sauté the pears in the butter and nutmeg until they are just soft, but not mushy, about 3 minutes. Set aside.

Visit PizzaIn5.com, where you'll find recipes, photos, videos, and instructional material. See page 53 for outdoor grill instructions.

2. **Prepare the walnuts:** In a small bowl toss together the nuts, maple syrup, salt, and pepper. Spread them out on a cookie sheet and bake for about 8 to 10 minutes at 350°F, until they are toasted and the syrup has caramelized. Set aside.

3. **Preheat a baking stone for 30 minutes to 450°F.** Sprinkle a pizza peel liberally with flour. Dust the surface of the refrigerated dough with flour and cut off a ½-pound (orange-size) piece. Dust with more flour and quickly shape it into a ball by stretching the surface of the dough around to the bottom on all four sides, rotating the ball a quarter-turn as you go.

4. **Stretch the dough:** Flatten the dough with your hands and/or a rolling pin on a work surface, or directly onto a wooden pizza peel, to produce a ⅛-inch-thick round. Dust with flour to keep the dough from adhering to the surface. Use a dough scraper to unstick the dough as needed, and transfer to a pizza peel if you haven't already stretched the dough on one. (See page 47 if you'd rather bake on a sheet pan.) When you're finished, the dough round should have enough flour under it to move easily when you shake the peel.

5. **Add the toppings:** Distribute the crumbled Gorgonzola and small chunks of cream cheese evenly over the dough, then the sautéed pears. Drizzle with maple syrup.

6. **Slide the pizza onto the preheated stone** (see Step 11, page 67): If

⌒⌒

TO PEEL OR NOT TO PEEL. Most of the color and a good deal of the fiber in pears and apples are in the skin, so we prefer to leave it on. If you are slicing the fruit thinly enough you will not notice it's there.

you're using a sheet pan, place it right on the stone. Check for doneness in 10 to 15 minutes and turn the pizza around in the oven if one side is browning faster than the other.

7. Allow to cool slightly, preferably on a wire cooling rack, cut into wedges, scatter the walnuts over the top, and serve.

Visit PizzaIn5.com, where you'll find recipes, photos, videos, and instructional material. See page 53 for outdoor grill instructions.

Hawaiian Pizza (Pineapple, Ham, and Macadamia Nuts)

We daresay that those who protest the mere idea of Hawaiian pizza have not tried our version, and we will make converts of you. The sweet pineapple, the salty, smoky ham, and the sharp cheddar are all in perfect harmony with the rich, toasted macadamia nuts.

Makes one 12-inch pizza

1/2 pound (orange-size portion) lean or gluten-free dough from pages 59–98

2 ounces thinly sliced prosciutto (smoked ham or precooked Canadian bacon work nicely as well)

4 ounces crushed pineapple, fresh or canned, drained of juice

2 ounces fresh mozzarella cheese, cut into 1/2-inch chunks (see Tips and Techniques, page 50)

2 ounces sharp cheddar or *ubriaco* cheese

1/4 cup chopped macadamia nuts

Drizzle of olive oil

Pinch of coarse salt

1 teaspoon finely chopped fresh sage

Flour, cornmeal, parchment paper, or rice flour for the pizza peel

1. **Prepare and measure** all toppings in advance.

2. **Preheat a baking stone at your oven's highest temperature for at least 30 minutes** (see "Why Such a Short Preheat," page 49). Sprinkle a pizza peel liberally with flour. Dust the surface of the refrigerated dough with flour and cut off a 1/2-pound (orange-size) piece. Dust with more flour and quickly shape it into a ball by stretching the

surface of the dough around to the bottom on all four sides, rotating the ball a quarter-turn as you go.

3. **Stretch the pizza crust:** Flatten the dough with your hands and/or a rolling pin on a work surface, or directly onto a wooden pizza peel, to produce a ⅛-inch-thick round. Dust with flour to keep the dough from adhering to the surface. Use a dough scraper to unstick the dough as needed, and transfer to a pizza peel if you haven't already stretched the dough on one. (See page 47 if you'd rather bake on a sheet pan.) When you're finished, the dough round should have enough flour under it to move easily when you shake the peel.

4. **Add the toppings:** Lay the ham down on the dough, so that it covers the entire surface, evenly distribute the pineapple, cheeses, and nuts over the top, then sprinkle with coarse salt and drizzle with olive oil.

5. **Slide the pizza onto the preheated stone** (see Step 11, page 67): If you're using a sheet pan, place it right on the stone. Check for doneness in 8 to 10 minutes and turn the pizza around in the oven if one side is browning faster than the other.

6. Allow to cool slightly, preferably on a wire cooling rack. Sprinkle with the sage, cut into wedges, and serve.

VARIATION: Fresh Fig, Candied Walnuts, and Port Glaze

In place of the crushed pineapple and macadamia nuts, use 8 fresh figs split in half lengthwise, 2 ounces of candied walnuts (see page 150), and 2 tablespoons port glaze (recipe follows) drizzled over the top before baking. For the port glaze: Simmer ½ cup of port wine in a small saucepan until it is reduced to 2 tablespoons, about 10 minutes.

Visit PizzaIn5.com, where you'll find recipes, photos, videos, and instructional material. See page 53 for outdoor grill instructions.

Apple, Ham, and Brie Tart

Apples in a savory tart? Absolutely. One typical combo in a savory fruit tart is blue cheese and pear, but this is the Upper Midwest, and apple-picking is a tradition for both our families in the autumn. We love the way the apples' sweetness picks up the sweetness of the brie and the ham. Use a firm, tart apple like Liberty or Granny Smith.

Makes one 12-inch tart

$1/2$ pound (orange-size portion) lean or gluten-free dough from pages 59–98 or Savory Brioche dough (page 107)

3 ounces Brie, Camembert, or *Rosso di Langa* cheese, cut into thin slices

1 firm apple, such as Liberty or Granny Smith variety, thinly sliced

3 ounces thinly sliced ham

$1/2$ teaspoon fresh thyme leaves (or $1/4$ teaspoon dried)

Flour, cornmeal, parchment paper, or rice flour for the pizza peel

1. **Prepare and measure** all toppings in advance.

2. **Preheat a baking stone at your oven's highest temperature for at least 30 minutes** (see "Why Such a Short Preheat," page 49). Sprinkle a pizza peel liberally with flour. Dust the surface of the refrigerated dough with flour and cut off a $1/2$-pound (orange-size) piece. Dust with more flour and quickly shape it into a ball by stretching the surface of the dough around to the bottom on all four sides, rotating the ball a quarter-turn as you go.

3. **Stretch the crust:** Flatten the dough with your hands and/or a rolling pin on a work surface, or directly onto a wooden pizza peel, to produce a 1/8-inch-thick round. Dust with flour to keep the dough from adhering to the surface. Use a dough scraper to unstick the dough as needed, and transfer to a pizza peel if you haven't already stretched the dough on one. (See page 47 if you'd rather bake on a sheet pan.) When you're finished, the dough round should have enough flour under it to move easily when you shake the peel.

4. **Add the toppings:** Distribute the cheese and apple slices over the dough and finish with the ham and thyme leaves. The cheese will not completely cover the surface of the dough.

5. **Slide the tart onto the preheated stone** (see Step 11, page 67): If you're using a sheet pan, place it right on the stone. Check for doneness in 8 to 10 minutes and turn the tart around in the oven if one side is browning faster than the other.

6. Allow to cool slightly, preferably on a wire cooling rack. Cut into wedges and serve with a crisp white wine.

VARIATION: Fresh Blackberries, Peach, Lavender, and Rosemary
Replace the apple and ham with 1/2 cup blackberries and 1/2 cup of peaches cut into small chunks, and place them over the Brie. Sprinkle 1 teaspoon chopped lavender and 2 teaspoons rosemary over the top. Drizzle with 2 tablespoons of honey and sprinkle with salt and pepper. Bake as above.

Visit PizzaIn5.com, where you'll find recipes, photos, videos, and instructional material. See page 53 for outdoor grill instructions.

Balthazar Goat Cheese and Onion Pizzette (Little Pizza-Tarts)

"These pizzettes were inspired by a savory tart that my cousin, chef Riad Nasr, serves at Balthazar in New York City. It is a mix of quintessentially French bistro flavors: caramelized onions, goat cheese, and thyme. They go well with many of our crusts but my two favorites are the Cornmeal Olive Oil and the Savory Brioche dough."—Zoë

Makes six 4-inch pizzettes

1 pound (grapefruit-size) lean or gluten-free dough from pages 59–98 or Savory Brioche dough (page 107)

2 tablespoons olive oil

2 medium yellow onions, peeled, cut into ⅛-inch-thick slices

1 bay leaf

2 teaspoons fresh thyme (or 1 teaspoon dried)

Salt and freshly ground black pepper to taste

4 ounces soft *chèvre*, at room temperature

4 ounces cream cheese, at room temperature

1 egg yolk

1. In a skillet over medium-low heat, add the olive oil, onions, bay leaf, thyme, salt, and pepper. Cook slowly, stirring occasionally, until the onions are golden. This may take 20 to 30 minutes. If the pan gets too dry, add some water to the onions, 2 tablespoons at a time.

2. In a small bowl mix together the cheeses and the egg yolk until smooth. Set aside.

3. **Preheat the oven to 475°F,** with the racks in the center and top third of the oven. Grease two baking sheets. Dust the surface of the refrigerated dough with flour and cut off a 1-pound (grapefruit-size) piece. Dust with more flour and quickly shape it into a ball by stretching the surface of the dough around to the bottom on all four sides, rotating the ball a quarter-turn as you go. Divide the dough into 6 equal portions and form into balls.

4. **Stretch the pizzette crusts:** Flatten each piece of dough with your hands and/or a rolling pin on a work surface (or shape the disk by hand, see page 42) to produce a $1/8$-inch-thick round. Dust with flour to keep the dough from adhering to the surface. Use a dough scraper to unstick the dough as needed, and transfer to the prepared baking sheets.

5. **Add the toppings:** Distribute the goat cheese mixture equally among the 6 dough rounds, spreading evenly, then add the onions.

6. **Place the baking sheets in the preheated oven**. Check for doneness in 10 minutes; at this time, turn the baking sheets around in the oven if one side of the pizzettes is browning faster than the other and switch the pans from the top and the bottom rack. It may take up to 5 minutes more in the oven.

7. Allow to cool, preferably on a wire cooling rack. Serve warm, not hot.

VARIATION: Caramelized Onions, Sautéed Potatoes, and Fresh Pecorino
Add 2 tablespoons of wine to the onion mixture while caramelizing. Once the onions are cooked, remove them from the pan and set aside. Add

Visit PizzaIn5.com, where you'll find recipes, photos, videos, and instructional material. See page 53 for outdoor grill instructions.

1 tablespoon olive oil to the same pan and sauté 1 thinly sliced potato for about 3 minutes, just to soften. Replace the cheese mixture with 3 ounces of grated pecorino cheese (or any other hard grating cheese). Roll out the pizzettes and distribute the toppings evenly over them, and sprinkle with salt and pepper. Bake as above.

Individual Breakfast Pizzas

Take the ever-loved breakfast combo of bacon and eggs, bake them on a crisp pizza crust, and you have an exciting twist on tradition. Shake it up a bit with sausage, Canadian bacon, or even *huevos rancheros* toppings. These pizzas are a quick, easy, and fun way to eat a traditional breakfast. See the variations below for different flavor combinations, and how to bake the pizzas in muffin cups for a more festive look.

Makes six 4-inch pizzas

1 pound (grapefruit-size portion) lean or gluten-free dough from pages 59–98 or
    Savory Brioche dough (page 107)
6 strips of bacon (or breakfast sausage or Canadian bacon)
6 ounces of cheddar cheese (or your favorite), shredded
6 large eggs
Salt and freshly ground pepper to taste
Butter or oil for greasing the pans

1. Prepare and measure all toppings in advance. Render the bacon, sausage, or Canadian bacon, break it up into pieces, and set aside.

2. **Preheat the oven to 475°F,** with the racks in the center and top third of the oven. Grease two baking sheets. Dust the surface of the refrigerated dough with flour and cut off a 1-pound (grapefruit-size) piece. Dust with more flour and quickly shape it into a ball by stretching the surface of the dough around to the bottom on all four sides, rotating the ball a quarter-turn as you go. Divide the dough into 6 equal portions and form them into balls.

3. **Roll out and stretch the crusts:** Flatten each piece of dough with your hands and/or a rolling pin on a work surface to produce a 1/8-inch-thick round. Dust with flour to keep the dough from adhering to the surface. Use a dough scraper to unstick the dough as needed. Transfer to the prepared baking sheets.

4. **Add the toppings:** Distribute the cheese evenly among the 6 dough rounds, add the bacon, then crack an egg over the top of each. Season with salt and pepper.

5. **Place the baking sheets in the preheated oven.** Check for doneness in 5 to 8 minutes; at this time, turn the baking sheets around in the oven if one side of the pizzas is browning faster than the other. It may take up to 5 minutes more in the oven.

6. Serve hot from the oven.

VARIATION: Pizza Lorraine
For a riff on the traditional quiche, replace the cheddar cheese with Gruyère and add a pinch of nutmeg and 1/2 teaspoon minced scallions or chives to the top of the egg when it comes out of the oven.

VARIATION: Pizza *Huevos Rancheros* (Mexican Ranch-Style Eggs)
Once the pizza comes out of the oven add to each: 2 tablespoons drained cooked or canned black beans, 2 tablespoons salsa, and 1 tablespoon sour cream or *crema fresca*.

VARIATION: Spinach and Feta
Replace the cheddar cheese with feta and add 2 tablespoons cooked, drained spinach to each of the pizzas before cracking the egg over the top.

VARIATION: Pesto, Fresh Tomato, Pecorino, and Prosciutto
Replace all the toppings with 4 tablespoons pesto (see page 114), 1 large ripe tomato, diced, 3 ounces shredded aged pecorino, and 6 thin slices of prosciutto. Distribute the toppings evenly among the pizzas and crack an egg over the top of each before baking.

VARIATION: Pizza in a Cup
To create a more festive breakfast treat try baking the individual pizzas in muffin pans. Grease the pans and lay the dough into the wells. Layer the ingredients into the dough cups, crack the egg over the top of each, and bake as directed above. (See photo in the color insert.) Don't overfill these, or the contents will spill out of the cups.

Visit PizzaIn5.com, where you'll find recipes, photos, videos, and instructional material. See page 53 for outdoor grill instructions.

Bacon and Spinach Pizza

Who doesn't love bacon? We even know a few vegetarians who'll make an exception for this savory treat. This rich pie uses sour cream and home-made bacon bits as the canvas for sautéed baby spinach. It is perfect for breakfast (especially if you add an egg broken over the top—see sidebar, page 166), or as dinner with a cold beer.

Makes one 12-inch pizza

$^{1}/_{2}$ pound (orange-size portion) lean or gluten-free dough from pages 59–98
4 slices thick-style bacon
1 shallot, finely minced (or $^{1}/_{2}$ small white onion)
3 cups fresh baby spinach, washed and dried (or 1 cup frozen spinach, defrosted and drained of extra liquid)
Salt and freshly ground black pepper to taste
$^{1}/_{3}$ cup sour cream (full-fat or low-fat), or Béchamel Sauce (page 117)
1 tablespoon chives, finely chopped
Flour, cornmeal, parchment paper, or rice flour for the pizza peel

1. **Prepare and measure** all toppings in advance.

2. Slowly cook the bacon in a large skillet over medium-low heat, until it is well cooked, but not yet crispy, which will take about 10 to 15 minutes depending on the thickness of the bacon. Drain the bacon on paper towels and reserve 2 tablespoons of the bacon fat in the skillet. Add the shallots to the bacon fat and sauté over medium heat until they are soft. Add the spinach, salt, and pepper and cook for about 1 minute. Remove from heat and set aside.

3. Crumble 3 of the bacon strips and add them to the sour cream.

4. **Preheat a baking stone at your oven's highest temperature for at least 30 minutes** (see "Why Such a Short Preheat," page 49). Sprinkle a pizza peel liberally with flour. Dust the surface of the refrigerated dough with flour and cut off a $1/2$-pound (orange-size) piece. Dust with more flour and quickly shape it into a ball by stretching the surface of the dough around to the bottom on all four sides, rotating the ball a quarter-turn as you go.

5. **Stretch the pizza crust:** Flatten the dough with your hands and/or a rolling pin on a work surface, or directly onto a wooden pizza peel, to produce a $1/8$-inch-thick round. Dust with flour to keep the dough from adhering to the surface. Use a dough scraper to unstick the dough as needed, and transfer to a pizza peel if you haven't already stretched the dough on one. (See page 47 if you'd rather bake on a sheet pan.) When you're finished, the dough round should have enough flour under it to move easily when you shake the peel.

6. **Add the toppings:** Spread the sour cream–bacon mixture over the dough, then add the sautéed spinach.

7. **Slide the pizza onto the preheated stone** (see Step 11, page 67): If you're using a sheet pan, place it right on the stone. Check for doneness in 8 to 10 minutes and turn the pizza around in the oven if one side is browning faster than the other.

Visit PizzaIn5.com, where you'll find recipes, photos, videos, and instructional material. See page 53 for outdoor grill instructions.

8. Break up the last piece of bacon and sprinkle it and the chives over the top. Allow to cool slightly, preferably on a wire cooling rack. Cut into wedges and serve.

VARIATION: Bacon and Egg Breakfast Pizza

Just after sliding the pizza into the oven, crack an egg or two over the top (see sidebar, page 166) and bake as usual.

Provençal Onion Tart with Cracked Egg and Anchovy

We both love the Provence region in the south of France, where steady streams of Italian immigrants have ensured that the pizza is always excellent. There are some wonderful surprises in Provençal pizza, such as this marvelous onion tart enhanced by an egg just before baking. The result is a wonderful sunny-side up egg. You won't be able to resist mopping up the soft yolk with the crust—the effect is rich and decadent.

The licorice flavors of anise are typical in Provençal cooking, and they work beautifully in this tart. If fennel bulb is available where you live, you can use it in place of some of the onion, and that will provide a beguiling hint of licorice.

Makes one 12-inch thin-crusted tart

$^{1}/_{2}$ pound (orange-size portion) lean or gluten-free dough from pages 59–98

1 tablespoon olive oil

2 medium onions, finely chopped (or use one onion and $^{1}/_{2}$ fennel bulb, chopped)

2 anchovy fillets, cut into short lengths

$^{1}/_{2}$ teaspoon anise seeds

$^{1}/_{2}$ teaspoon fresh thyme leaves (or $^{1}/_{4}$ teaspoon dried)

1 egg

Salt and freshly ground pepper

Pinch of coarse salt for sprinkling to taste

Flour, cornmeal, parchment paper, or rice flour for the pizza peel

Visit PizzaIn5.com, where you'll find recipes, photos, videos, and instructional material. See page 53 for outdoor grill instructions.

1. **Prepare and measure** all toppings in advance.

2. Sauté the onion (and fennel, if using) in the oil over medium heat, until it just begins to caramelize.

3. **Preheat a baking stone at your oven's highest temperature for at least 30 minutes** (see "Why Such a Short Preheat," page 49). Sprinkle a pizza peel liberally with flour. Dust the surface of the refrigerated dough with flour and cut off a $\frac{1}{2}$-pound (orange-size) piece. Dust with more flour and quickly shape it into a ball by stretching the surface of the dough around to the bottom on all four sides, rotating the ball a quarter-turn as you go.

4. **Stretch the crust:** Flatten the dough with your hands and/or a rolling pin on a work surface, or directly onto a wooden pizza peel, to produce a $\frac{1}{8}$-inch-thick round. Dust with flour to keep the dough from adhering to the surface. Use a dough scraper to unstick the dough as needed, and transfer to a pizza peel if you haven't already stretched the dough on one. (See page 47 if you'd rather bake on a sheet pan). When you're finished, the dough round should have enough flour under it to move easily when you shake the peel.

5. **Add the toppings:** Scatter the onion (and fennel, if using), anchovy, anise, and thyme over the dough.

෴

GETTING A PERFECT SOFT-COOKED EGG: In a 500°F oven, a cracked egg will bake to soft-boiled perfection during the pizza's baking time, but if your oven goes to 550°F, you need to wait 2 to 4 minutes before cracking the egg, otherwise it will be hard-cooked. Experiment with your oven to find the best timing.

6. **Slide the tart onto the preheated stone** (see Step 11, page 67): If you're using a sheet pan, place it right on the stone.

7. **Crack an egg on top,** right in the center of the tart; season with salt and pepper (see sidebar, page 166). Don't try to put the egg on before sliding the tart into the oven, or it will fall off during the slide, and don't use a convection oven, or the yolk will overcook.

8. Check for doneness in 8 to 10 minutes and turn the pizza around in the oven if one side is browning faster than the other.

9. Allow to cool slightly, preferably on a wire cooling rack. Cut into wedges and serve.

Visit PizzaIn5.com, where you'll find recipes, photos, videos, and instructional material. See page 53 for outdoor grill instructions.

Breakfast Pizza with Prosciutto, Cheese, and Egg

Here's breakfast inspired by a staple of the Italian rustic tradition: the *frittata*. In a traditional frittata, you start on the stovetop in a skillet with something suspiciously similar to an omelet, but finish under the broiler. We start the pizza in the oven and finish under the broiler—it's a snap.

Makes one 12-inch pizza

$1/2$ pound (orange-size portion) lean or gluten-free dough from pages 59–98 or Savory Brioche dough (page 107)
4 eggs
Salt and freshly ground black pepper to taste
4 ounces mozzarella, cheddar, Colby, or Swiss cheese, grated or sliced
2 ounces prosciutto, or other thinly sliced ham, cut into bite-size pieces
1 tablespoon grated Parmigiano-Reggiano cheese
Flour, cornmeal, parchment paper, or rice flour for the pizza peel

1. **Prepare and measure** all toppings in advance.

2. **Preheat a 12-inch cast-iron skillet for 30 minutes in an oven set at 450°F.** Sprinkle a pizza peel or other work surface liberally with flour. Dust the surface of the refrigerated dough with flour and cut off a $1/2$-pound (orange-size) piece. Dust with more flour and quickly shape it into a ball by stretching the surface of the dough around to the bottom on all four sides, rotating the ball a quarter-turn as you go.

3. **Stretch a crust large enough to fit the bottom of your skillet:** Flatten the dough with your hands and/or a rolling pin on a work surface, or

a pizza peel, to produce a $1/8$-inch-thick round. Dust with flour to keep the dough from adhering to the surface. Use a dough scraper to unstick the dough as needed.

4. **Bake the crust "blind":** Open the oven door, slide out the shelf, and position the skillet so that you can drop or slide the dough into the bottom without burning yourself. Dock (puncture) the dough all over with the tines of a fork. Bake for 5 minutes. If bubbles form, poke them with a long-handled fork to deflate.

5. While the crust is baking, lightly beat the eggs and season with salt and pepper. When the crust is at the 5-minute mark, pour the beaten eggs over the dough. They will distribute unevenly, and some may slip under the crust. Distribute the softer cheese over the dough, then the prosciutto, and finish with the Parmigiano.

6. **Complete the baking:** Slide the skillet back into the oven and check for doneness in 5 minutes. It may take up to 5 minutes more in the oven for the visible crust to brown, but you'll still need to broil briefly to finish the eggs.

7. **Run under the broiler** until the egg surface browns and the eggs are almost set, but don't overdo it or they'll be dry—1 to 2 minutes should be enough. The eggs will continue to set for another 3 minutes after removing the pan from the heat.

8. Cut the frittata into wedges and serve. Accompany with Mimosas and a fruit salad at a lazy Sunday afternoon brunch.

Visit PizzaIn5.com, where you'll find recipes, photos, videos, and instructional material. See page 53 for outdoor grill instructions.

Stovetop Pizza

You have the dough in the refrigerator, but you're in a pinch for time and don't want to preheat your oven. Instead, you can make a pizza on the stove in less than five minutes. The bottom crust is crunchy and the top is toasted for just a minute under the broiler to give it that wood-fired oven feel— simple and fast.

Makes one 8-inch pizza

¼-pound (peach-size portion) lean or gluten-free dough from pages 59–98
2 tablespoons tomato topping (see page 109)
1 ounce mozzarella cheese, thinly sliced or grated
1 teaspoon olive oil

1. **Prepare and measure** all toppings in advance.

2. **Heat an 8-inch cast-iron skillet over medium heat on the stove.** Dust the surface of the refrigerated dough with flour and cut off a ¼-pound (peach-size) piece. Dust with more flour and quickly shape it into a ball by stretching the surface of the dough around to the bottom on all four sides, rotating the ball a quarter-turn as you go.

3. **Stretch the pizza crust:** Flatten the dough with your hands and/or a rolling pin on a work surface, or directly onto a wooden pizza peel, to produce a ⅛-inch-thick round. Dust with flour to keep the dough from adhering to the surface. Use a dough scraper to unstick

the dough as needed, and transfer to the preheated pan. Some of the dough may go up the sides.

4. **Add the toppings:** Quickly spread the tomato over the dough, then the cheese and oil.

5. Cover the skillet and cook for about 4 minutes; be sure not to lift the lid, unless you smell scorching.

6. **Turn on the broiler,** remove the lid, and toast the pizza for 1 to 2 minutes to get a lovely crisp top crust. Be careful not to overdo it or the toppings will burn. Remove from the skillet with a spatula.

7. Allow to cool slightly, preferably on a wire cooling rack. Cut into wedges and serve.

Visit PizzaIn5.com, where you'll find recipes, photos, videos, and instructional material. See page 53 for outdoor grill instructions.

8

THICK-CRUST PIZZA, FOCACCIA, AND FLATBREADS

Thick-Crusted Sicilian-Style Pizza with Onions (*Sfinciuni*)

"Thick-crusted, square sfinciuni *(sfin-choóny) can be found all over Italy, from Naples to Venice, but it finds its origins in Sicily. It became my family's daily lunch of choice, with as many toppings to choose from as there are bakeries that sell it. The traditional Sicilian version has very little beyond a thin layer of tomato and a sprinkle of pecorino, or perhaps anchovies. Once you leave Sicily there seem to be no rules about what to put on top. One of our favorites was piled high with rings of sweet onions."*—Zoë (see color insert)

Makes one 13 × 18-inch pizza

2 pounds (small-cantaloupe size) portion lean dough (pages 59–95) or Savory
    Brioche dough (page 107)
6 ounces mozzarella cheese, cut into very thin slices or shredded
3/4 cup tomato topping of your choice (see page 109)
3 ounces finely grated pecorino Romano cheese

2 large onions, sliced into thin rounds

2 tablespoons olive oil, plus more for greasing the pan

Salt to taste

Anchovies (optional)

1. **Preheat the oven to 500°F.** Generously grease a 13 × 18-inch baking sheet pan with olive oil. Dust the surface of the refrigerated dough with flour and cut off a 2-pound (small-cantaloupe size) piece. Dust with more flour and quickly shape it into a ball by stretching the surface of the dough around to the bottom on all four sides, rotating the ball a quarter-turn as you go.

2. **Stretch the pizza crust:** Flatten the dough with your hands on the greased surface of the pan to produce a ¼-inch-thick rectangle; it should eventually fit right to the edges of the pan. Poking the dough with your fingertips and stretching it with the palms of your hands will help stretch it out. Once the dough is stretched to the size of the pan, let it rest for 15 minutes.

3. **Add the toppings:** Spread the mozzarella evenly over the dough, and then add the tomato. Scatter the pecorino over the top along with the onions, a drizzle of olive oil, and a sprinkle of salt.

4. **Place the baking sheet into the preheated oven:** Check for doneness in 20 minutes and turn the pizza around in the oven if one side is browning faster than the other. It may take up to 5 more minutes in the oven.

5. Allow to cool slightly, cut into squares, and serve.

VARIATIONS:

Brooklyn Style: No onions, just plain and simple.

Bolognese: Replace the tomato sauce with 1½ cups Bolognese (Meat) Sauce (page 112); onions are optional. Because of the chunkiness of this sauce it requires twice as much.

Tapenade: Replace the tomato and onions with 1 cup of tapenade (page 213).

Visit PizzaIn5.com, where you'll find recipes, photos, videos, and instructional material. See page 53 for outdoor grill instructions.

Thick-Crusted Roman Eggplant Pizza

"In Rome, I watched pizzaioli *cut slices of savory eggplant pizza from long ovals; they'd sell it by having you estimate length but then weigh it for the final price. The slices of grilled eggplant look as good as they taste (see photo). As in New York, the Romans eat pizza by biting into two layers like a sandwich, but unlike New Yorkers, they slap two squares together instead of folding a wedge in half."*—Jeff

Makes one 16-inch-long oval pizza

1 pound (grapefruit-size portion) lean dough (pages 59–95)

$^{1}/_{3}$ cup tomato topping of your choice (see page 109)

$^{1}/_{2}$ small eggplant, sliced into $^{1}/_{8}$-inch-thick rounds, and brushed generously with olive oil

Salt for the eggplant

3 ounces mozzarella or other medium-soft cheese, cut into $^{1}/_{2}$-inch chunks (see Tips and Techniques, page 50)

Olive oil for greasing the baking sheet

1. **Prepare and measure** all toppings in advance. Generously grease a heavy baking sheet with olive oil.

2. Salt the eggplant to taste, and then grill the slices briefly over direct medium heat on a gas or wood-fired grill for about 3 to 5 minutes per side.

3. **Preheat a baking stone at your oven's highest temperature for at least 30 minutes** (see "Why Such a Short Preheat," page 49). Sprinkle a work surface liberally with flour.

Dust the surface of the refrigerated dough with flour and cut off a 1-pound (grapefruit-size) piece. Dust with more flour and quickly shape it into a ball by stretching the surface of the dough around to the bottom on all four sides, rotating the ball a quarter-turn as you go.

4. **Roll out and stretch the pizza crust into an elongated oval** (see Pizza Bianca, page 201) about ¼ inch thick, and transfer to the prepared sheet pan.

5. **Add the toppings:** Spread the tomato topping over the dough, then distribute the cheese and eggplant.

6. **Place the baking sheet in the oven,** and check for doneness in 8 to 10 minutes. Turn the pan around in the oven if one side is browning faster than the other. It may take up to 5 minutes more in the oven.

7. Allow to cool slightly, preferably on a wire cooling rack. Cut into squares and serve. Make a pizza sandwich in the Roman style by sticking the cheesy sides of two squares together (see color insert).

Visit PizzaIn5.com, where you'll find recipes, photos, videos, and instructional material. See page 53 for outdoor grill instructions.

Coca (Catalan Flatbread) with Manchego, Leeks, Sardines, and Red Pepper

Coca, the flatbread from the Catalonia region of Spain, differs from Italian and other flatbreads in subtle but important ways. Caramelized onions seem to show up on many of them, along with red peppers and things like Mediterranean sardines (we substitute canned for hard-to-find fresh sardines, or you could even use anchovy fillets). On our last book tour, we had a fantastic *coca* at a Catalan place in San Francisco, where they swapped caramelized leeks for the caramelized onions, which was a brilliant choice—richer yet more refined than onions.

Makes one 12-inch flatbread

1 pound (grapefruit-size portion) lean or gluten-free dough from pages 59–98
3 tablespoons olive oil, plus more for greasing the pan

1 leek (white part only), halved lengthwise, well rinsed, then thinly sliced crosswise

$1/2$ teaspoon salt

1 teaspoon brown sugar

2 tablespoons water

3 ounces Manchego cheese (or other medium-firm cheese), coarsely grated

6 small canned sardines packed in olive oil (anchovy fillets can be substituted)

$1/4$ teaspoon dried thyme ($1/2$ teaspoon chopped fresh)

$1/4$ red bell pepper, seeded, quartered, and sliced into very thin strips

❧

IF YOU'RE NOT A SARDINE FAN, the *coca* works beautifully with clams (see page 17) or small shrimp. Another great option that fits the Spanish theme is Spanish-style *chorizo*, sliced thin and rendered of some of its fat before using.

1. **Prepare and measure** all toppings in advance.

2. Heat the olive oil in a large skillet on medium-low heat. Add the sliced leek, salt, sugar, and water and cook for about 25 minutes, stirring occasionally, until the leeks caramelize; most of the liquid will evaporate.

3. Grease a heavy baking sheet with olive oil and set aside.

4. **Preheat a baking stone at your oven's highest temperature for at least 30 minutes** (see "Why Such a Short Preheat," page 49). Sprinkle a work surface liberally with flour. Dust the surface of the refrigerated dough with flour and cut off a 1-pound (grapefruit-size) piece. Dust with more flour and quickly shape it into a ball by stretching the surface of the dough around to the bottom on all four sides, rotating the ball a quarter-turn as you go.

5. **Stretch the flatbread crust:** Flatten the dough with your hands and a rolling pin on a work surface, or directly onto a wooden pizza peel, to produce a $1/4$-inch-thick round. Dust with flour to keep the dough from adhering to the surface. Use a dough scraper to unstick the dough as needed, and transfer to the prepared baking sheet.

6. **Add the toppings:** Set the dough onto the baking sheet, and distribute the cheese, the reserved leeks, sardines, and thyme over the top. Then add the red pepper strips in crisscross patterns.

Visit PizzaIn5.com, where you'll find recipes, photos, videos, and instructional material. See page 53 for outdoor grill instructions.

7. **Place the baking sheet on the preheated stone.** Bake for 8 to 10 minutes, and turn the pan around in the oven if one side is browning faster than the other. It may take up to 5 minutes more in the oven.

8. Allow to cool slightly, preferably on a wire cooling rack. Cut into wedges and serve.

Spanish Galician Potato Soup with Greens and Chorizo (*Caldo Galego*)

"Years ago I studied for a while in the north of Spain, close to the region of Galicia. You can still hear the Galician language (which more closely resembles Portuguese than Spanish), and a distinctive regional cuisine flourishes. There's deep pride for the local culture—one of my classmates was Galician and only answered to 'Gallo' (kind of like a Texan wanting to be called 'Tex'—he was a bit of a character). I like to think that Gallo and his family would sit down during winter break and eat hearty soups like this one. If you can't get Spanish-style chorizo, *the Mexican variety works nicely, or the Portuguese-style* linguiça *sausage (or any sausage you like). If you puree the soup before adding the sausage, the result will be a little closer to a French-style* potage, *but the original is the more rustic creation."*—Jeff

Serves 6 to 8

3 or 4 large *chorizo* or *linguiça* sausages (1 pound)

3 tablespoons olive oil

1 large onion, diced

3 large garlic cloves, minced

2 teaspoons paprika

8 cups water, vegetable stock, beef stock, or chicken stock

5 large Yukon gold potatoes (about 2 pounds) unpeeled, cut in $1/2$-inch dice

∽

THE RECIPE WORKS WELL WITH MANY KINDS OF GREEN VEGETABLES. The closest you can come to traditional *caldo galego* is to use broccoli rabe stems and greens, now widely available in the United States. It's a close cousin to a local Galician green called *grelo*, and it imparts a nice astringency to the soup. But you can experiment with anything you like as the green part of the dish, including ordinary broccoli.

Visit PizzaIn5.com, where you'll find recipes, photos, videos, and instructional material. See page 53 for outdoor grill instructions.

3 cups chopped broccoli rabe (discard the toughest stems but most are quite edible), kale, or spinach, tightly packed

1 bay leaf

2 teaspoons salt (decrease if using salty stock)

Freshly ground black pepper to taste

1. **Prepare the sausages—grill or pan-render:** To grill the sausages whole, cook for them about 10 minutes, turning once. When cooked through, cut them lengthwise, slice crosswise, and add to the soup at the end. **For an even richer flavor,** halve and slice the sausages and then render in the soup pot over medium heat. Then use the rendered fat to sauté the onion and garlic in Step 2. Set the cooked sausages aside.

2. If using rendered fat, decrease the oil by 1 tablespoon and heat the oil/fat in a heavy 6-quart saucepan over medium heat. Add the onion and sauté until it begins to brown. Add the garlic and paprika and cook briefly, just until the garlic begins to brown.

3. Add the water or stock, potatoes, broccoli rabe, and the bay leaf and simmer, partly covered, for about 30 minutes, or until potatoes and greens are soft. If you're using spinach, add it later in the simmer— wait until the potatoes are almost soft.

4. Remove the bay leaf, add salt and pepper, taste and adjust the seasonings as needed. Cool and run through the food processor or use an immersion blender right in the pot, before adding the sausage.

5. Add sausage and serve with fresh flatbreads. Traditional Galician breads often have lots of rye and caraway in them—think northern Europe, not the Spanish Mediterranean (see seeded rye pita variation, page 201).

Leek, Herbes de Provence, and Garlic Focaccia

This outstanding French combination of ingredients is fragrant and delicious on flatbread. *Herbes de Provence* is a mixture of equal parts savory, fennel, basil, rosemary, marjoram, and thyme. Often lavender is included and adds a wonderful scent and flavor to the mix. You can find this blend in most groceries or create your own. The flowery herbs go perfectly with the pungent flavor of leeks and garlic.

Makes one 10-inch focaccia

$^3/_4$ pound (large orange-size portion) lean or gluten-free dough from pages 59–98
    or Savory Brioche dough (page 107)
5 tablespoons olive oil
1 leek (white part only), halved lengthwise, well rinsed, and thinly sliced crosswise
2 tablespoons *herbes de Provence*
3 garlic cloves, thinly sliced
1 teaspoon capers
Salt and freshly ground black pepper to taste
$^1/_4$ cup white wine

1. **Prepare the leeks:** In a skillet over medium low heat, add
    2 tablespoons of the olive oil, leeks, herbs, garlic, capers, salt, pepper,
    and white wine. Cook slowly until the leeks are soft, but not brown.
    Allow to cool slightly.

2. **Preheat the oven to 450°F.** Rub 2 tablespoons of the olive oil in the
    bottom of a pie tin, set aside. Dust the surface of the refrigerated
    dough with flour and cut off a $^3/_4$-pound (large orange-size) piece.

Visit PizzaIn5.com, where you'll find recipes, photos, videos, and instructional material. See page 53 for outdoor grill instructions.

Dust with more flour and quickly shape it into a ball by stretching the surface of the dough around to the bottom on all four sides, rotating the ball a quarter-turn as you go.

3. **Stretch the focaccia dough:** Flatten the dough with your hands and/or a rolling pin on a work surface, or directly onto the wooden pizza peel, to produce a ½-inch-thick round. Dust with flour to keep the dough from adhering to the surface. Use a dough scraper to unstick the dough as needed, and transfer to the prepared pie plate. Drizzle with 1 tablespoon olive oil and dimple the surface so the oil won't run off the top.

4. **Add the toppings:** Spread the leek mixture over the dough and allow to rest for 20 minutes. Just before baking press your fingers into the dough to dimple it throughout; this prevents the toppings from popping off when baking.

5. **Place the pie tin in the oven on the middle rack:** Check for doneness in 15 minutes, then turn the focaccia around in the oven if one side is browning faster than the other. It may take up to 5 minutes more in the oven.

6. Remove the focaccia from the pie tin and allow to cool slightly, preferably on a wire cooling rack. Cut into wedges and serve.

Moroccan Flatbread

Salty preserved lemons, cured olives, and the spice of *harissa*, a hot North African chili paste, are a traditional and exciting combination in Moroccan kitchens. This thick-style flatbread is lovely with soups, salads, or dips.

Makes one 10-inch flatbread

3/4 pound (large orange-size portion) lean or gluten-free dough (pages 59–98) or Savory Brioche dough (page 107)

4 tablespoons olive oil

2 teaspoons *harissa* paste (or make your own by blending together 1 garlic clove, 1/4 teaspoon cayenne pepper, 1/4 teaspoon ground ancho chili powder, 1/4 teaspoon paprika, and 1 teaspoon olive oil)

2 tablespoons finely chopped preserved lemon, store-bought or homemade (available in ethnic markets, or make your own; see sidebar, page 186)

1/4 cup chopped cured olives

1. **Prepare and measure** all toppings in advance.

2. **Preheat the oven to 450°F.** Rub 2 tablespoons of the olive oil in the bottom of a pie tin and set aside. Dust the surface of the refrigerated dough with flour and cut off a 3/4-pound (large orange-size) piece. Dust with more flour and quickly shape it into a ball by stretching the surface of the dough around to the bottom on all four sides, rotating the ball a quarter-turn as you go.

Visit PizzaIn5.com, where you'll find recipes, photos, videos, and instructional material. See page 53 for outdoor grill instructions.

∾

PRESERVED LEMON

Preserved lemons are available in some ethnic markets. It's easy to create these salty lemons for Moroccan dishes, but you need to set them aside to cure for several days. Wash and dry 5 to 6 lemons, and cut off the ends. Make 4 cuts down the length of the lemon, as if you are going to cut it in quarters, but only cut through the peel, not the flesh of the fruit. Fill each of the cuts with kosher salt. In a sterilized canning jar add 2 tablespoons of kosher salt. Press the first lemon into the jar, squashing it to the bottom. Cover with 2 more tablespoons of salt. Press the next lemon in and cover with more salt. Continue until the jar is filled. If you have any lemons left, set them aside. They may fit once the lemons start to break down in a few days and can be added then. The lemons should be very tightly packed with

(continued)

3. **Roll out and stretch the dough:** Flatten the dough with your hands and/or a rolling pin on a work surface to produce a $1/2$-inch-thick round. Dust with flour to keep the dough from adhering to the surface. Use a dough scraper to unstick the dough as needed, transfer to the prepared pie plate, drizzle with 1 tablespoon olive oil, and dimple the surface so the oil won't run off the top (see photos, page 184).

4. **Add the toppings:** In a small bowl combine the remaining olive oil and *harissa* paste. Spread the mixture over the dough, then scatter the chopped lemons and cured olives on top. Allow the dough to rest for 20 minutes.

5. Just before baking: Dimple the dough with your finger tips to prevent it from puffing too much while baking.

6. **Place the pie tin into the oven on the middle rack:** Check for doneness in 15 minutes and turn the flatbread

around in the oven if one side is browning faster than the other. It may take up to five more minutes in the oven.

7. Remove the flatbread from the pie tin and allow to cool slightly, preferably on a wire cooling rack. Cut into wedges and serve.

(continued)

salt and juice reaching the top of the jar. Set aside at room temperature for 2 days. You may need to turn the jar upside down to make sure the lemons are submerged in the salty juice.

Spinach and Ricotta "Piz-zone" (Pizza + Calzone)

"On our first night in Rome we were tired and hungry after traveling, so we went to the first restaurant we could find. It was not exactly the quaint little Italian place I'd envisioned, but the boys loved it because they had the World Cup playing on the television and they served this 'Piz-zone,' which combined their two favorite foods in one dish—pizza and calzone. One side was stuffed with spinach and fresh ricotta, while the other half was a flat pizza with sweet tomatoes, mozzarella, and a crispy crust. Happy boys make for happy travels!"—Zoë

Makes one 12-inch piz-zone

¾ pound (large orange-size portion) lean or gluten-free dough from pages 59–98

3 ounces ricotta cheese

½ cup cooked spinach or 1 roasted red bell pepper, cut into bite-size pieces (pages 207–208)

3 ounces mozzarella cheese, cut into ½-inch chunks (see Tips and Techniques, page 50)

¼ teaspoon ground nutmeg

Pinch of salt

3 tablespoons tomato topping (see page 109)

Olive oil for brushing

1 ounce grated Parmigiano-Reggiano for sprinkling

2 fresh basil leaves, torn or chiffonaded (see page 9)

Flour, cornmeal, parchment paper, or rice flour for the pizza peel

1. **Prepare and measure** all toppings in advance.

2. **Preheat a baking stone at your oven's highest temperature for at least 30 minutes** (see "Why Such a Short Preheat," page 49). Sprinkle a pizza peel liberally with flour. Dust the surface of the refrigerated dough with flour and cut off a ³/₄-pound (large orange-size) piece. Dust with more flour and quickly shape it into a ball by stretching the surface of the dough around to the bottom on all four sides, rotating the ball a quarter-turn as you go.

3. **Stretch the piz-zone crust:** Flatten the dough with your hands and/or a rolling pin on a work surface, or directly onto a wooden pizza peel, to produce a ¹/₈-inch-thick oval. Dust with flour to keep the dough from adhering to the surface. Use a dough scraper to unstick the dough as needed, and transfer to a pizza peel if you haven't already stretched the dough on one. (See page 47 if you'd rather bake on a sheet pan). When you're finished, the dough round should have enough flour under it to move easily when you shake the peel.

4. **Add the toppings:** On the half of the dough that is closest to the end of the pizza peel place the ricotta cheese, the spinach, 1 ounce of the

  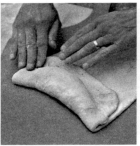 

mozzarella, the nutmeg, and salt, just off of the center line. Fold the short end over the fillings to reach the middle to create the calzone. Press the dough down to seal. On the other side, which is still flat, spread out the tomato and cover with the remaining mozzarella cheese. Paint the top of the calzone side with olive oil and sprinkle with the grated Parmigiano-Reggiano.

5. **Slide the piz-zone onto the preheated stone** (See Step 11, page 67): If you're using a sheet pan, place it right on the stone. Check for doneness in 8 to 10 minutes and turn the piz-zone around in the oven if one side is browning faster than the other.

6. Allow to cool slightly, preferably on a wire cooling rack. Top with basil, cut into wedges, and serve.

VARIATION: Pepperoni and Fresh Oregano
Add pepperoni to the open side of the pizza and replace the basil with fresh oregano. Bake as directed.

Chicago-Style Deep-Dish Pizza

There's no question that deep-dish pizza was invented in Chicago, although there is some dispute over which pizzeria came up with it first. The pizza varies around Chicago, but for all, the crust is remarkable for its tender, almost buttery flavor and its luscious golden color, courtesy of cornmeal. Baking the pizza in a butter-coated cake pan fries the outside edge and makes for a crispy crust.

Makes about one 8 × 2-inch deep-dish pizza or four 6 × 1-inch individual deep-dish pizzas

¾ pound (large orange-size portion) Cornmeal Olive Oil Dough (page 86), any lean dough (pages 59–95), or Savory Brioche dough (page 107)

4 large Italian sausages (about ¾ pound), cooked and broken into small pieces

1½ cups shredded mozzarella cheese

1 cup thick tomato sauce (Variation, page 110)

Butter for the pan

Cornmeal for the pan

1. **Prepare and measure** all toppings in advance.

2. **Preheat oven to 500°F.** Generously butter an 8 × 2-inch spring-form cake pan (or the smaller individual pans, see Chapter 3, page 33) and coat with cornmeal. Dust the surface of the refrigerated dough with flour and cut off a ¾-pound (large orange-size) piece. Dust with more flour and quickly shape it into a ball by stretching the surface of the dough around to the bottom on all four sides, rotating the ball a

quarter-turn as you go (if making individual pies, divide the dough into 4 pieces and shape into balls).

3. **Roll out and stretch the pizza crust:** Flatten the dough with your hands and a rolling pin on a work surface to produce a $\frac{1}{8}$-inch-thick round. Dust with flour to keep the dough from sticking to the surface. Use a dough scraper to unstick the dough as needed. Transfer to the cake pan. The dough should hang over the edge of the pan, which will prevent it from "slouching" while you fill it.

4. **Add the fillings:** Mix together the sausage and two-thirds of the cheese in a bowl. Spread the meat mixture onto the dough, then top with the sauce and the remaining cheese. Trim the overhanging dough with kitchen shears so there is about $\frac{1}{2}$ inch of dough that will flop down over the filling.

5. **Slide the pizza into the preheated oven. Reduce the oven temperature to 400°F.** Check for doneness in about 45 minutes (20 minutes for the individual pizzas). The pizza should be bubbling and the cheese evenly melted.

6. Allow to cool for about 10 minutes, preferably on a wire cooling rack. This allows the filling to set slightly before removing from the pan and slicing. When cooled, cut into wedges and serve.

Italian Torta

"One of my first jobs in a professional kitchen was with D'Amico Catering in Minneapolis, where we made an Italian torta, *stuffed to the rim with roasted vegetables and cheese. It was gorgeous and easily the most popular item on the menu. Despite its beauty this version is really very simple to create. The torta is a great side dish or vegetarian main course."*—Zoë

Makes one 8-inch torta

1 pound (grapefruit-size portion) Cornmeal Olive Oil Dough (page 86), Savory Brioche dough (page 107), or any lean dough (pages 59–95)

2 cups small button mushrooms, or your favorite mushrooms, cut into $^1/_2$-inch pieces

1 tablespoon olive oil

Salt and freshly ground black pepper to taste

4 cups shredded mozzarella

1 cup cooked spinach, fresh or frozen (thawed and liquid squeezed out)

2 large red bell peppers, roasted and quartered (see pages 207–208)

1 cup oil-packed, quartered artichoke hearts, drained, chopped into chunks

2 large yellow bell peppers, roasted and quartered (see pages 207–208)

12 *pepperoncini*, cut in half lengthwise

Butter for cake pan

Egg wash for the top crust (1 egg beaten with 1 tablespoon water)

1. **Prepare the toppings:** Sauté the mushrooms in the olive oil over medium low heat until soft. Add a tablespoon of water to the pan if they are sticking. Season with salt and pepper to taste.

Visit PizzaIn5.com, where you'll find recipes, photos, videos, and instructional material. See page 53 for outdoor grill instructions.

2. **On baking day, preheat the oven to 400°F.** Generously butter an 8-inch spring-form cake pan. Dust the surface of the refrigerated dough with flour and cut off a 1-pound (grapefruit-size) piece. Dust with more flour and quickly shape it into a ball by stretching the surface of the dough around to the bottom on all four sides, rotating the ball a quarter-turn as you go. Divide the ball by cutting off one-fourth of it.

3. **Stretch the torta crust:** Flatten the larger dough ball with your hands and/or a rolling pin on a work surface to produce a ⅛-inch-thick round. Dust with flour to keep the dough from sticking to the surface. Transfer the dough to the prepared cake pan. The dough should hang over the edge of the pan by about an inch, which will prevent it from "slouching" while you fill it.

4. **Add the fillings:** Evenly spread ½ cup of the mozzarella on the bottom of the crust. Cover the cheese with the sautéed mushrooms and top with ½ cup of the cheese. Repeat this layering with the spinach, red bell pepper, artichoke hearts, yellow bell pepper, and *pepperoncini*. Add the remaining cheese to the top. Trim the dough that is overhanging the pan with kitchen shears so there is about ½ inch of dough above the filling.

5. **Roll out and stretch the top crust:** Flatten the smaller dough ball with your hands and a rolling pin on a work surface to produce a ⅛-inch-thick round. Place the round over the filling. Fold the over-hanging bottom crust over the top crust, trim off the excess. (See

sidebar for decorative leaves.) Use a pastry brush to paint egg wash over the top crust.

6. **Slide the torta into the preheated oven:** Check for doneness in about 45 minutes; it should be golden brown.

7. Allow to cool for about 10 to 15 minutes, preferably on a wire rack. This will allow the filling to set slightly before removing from the pan. When cool, remove from the pan. Set on a serving platter and cut into wedges to serve.

DECORATIVE LEAVES Roll out a 2-ounce piece of dough into 1/8-inch-thick rectangle. Use a cookie cutter or sharp knife to cut out 8 to 12 leaves. Place the leaves on the top of the torta before baking.

Visit PizzaIn5.com, where you'll find recipes, photos, videos, and instructional material. See page 53 for outdoor grill instructions.

Pizza Spirals on a Stick

We originally made these for a TV demo at the Minnesota State Fair, where everything is served on a stick. It is a well-known fact that kids will eat just about anything if it is in the form of a lollipop. These cute pizzas are a nice way to sneak some variety into your kids' lunchboxes.

Makes twelve 2-inch pizza spirals

1/2 pound (orange-size portion) lean dough (pages 59–95) or Savory Brioche dough (page 107)
1/3 cup tomato topping (see page 109)
3 ounces mozzarella cheese, grated
Oil, butter, or parchment paper for the baking sheets
12 skewers for the pizza lollipops

1. **Prepare and measure** all toppings in advance. Prepare two baking sheets with oil, butter, or sheets of parchment.

2. **Preheat the oven to 450°F,** with racks in the center and top third of the oven. Dust the surface of the refrigerated dough with flour and cut off a 1/2-pound (orange-size) piece. Dust with more flour and quickly shape it into a ball by stretching the surface of the dough around to the bottom on all four sides, rotating the ball a quarter-turn as you go.

3. **Stretch the pizza crust:** Flatten the dough with your hands and a rolling pin on the work surface to produce a 1/8-inch-thick rectangle.

Dust with flour to keep the dough from adhering to the surface. Use a dough scraper to unstick the dough as needed.

4. **Add the toppings:** Spread the tomato over the dough, then add the cheese. Starting at the long end of the rectangle, roll the dough into a log. Pinch the seam closed. Stretch the dough out to 12 inches long and then, using a kitchen shears, cut 12 equal pieces from the log. Place them on the two prepared baking sheets.

5. **Place the pan into the preheated oven.** Check for doneness in 15 minutes and switch the pans from top to bottom if one is browning faster than the other. It may take up to 5 minutes more in the oven.

6. Allow to cool slightly, preferably on a wire cooling rack. For a more festive look, use skewers and poke them through the end of the spiral.

VARIATIONS:
Pepperoni: Add pepperoni before rolling up.
Pesto: Replace the tomato with pesto (page 114).
Ham and Cheese: Use 3 ounces of your favorite cheese and 3 ounces of thinly sliced ham instead of the pizza toppings.

9

PITA AND DIPS, PLUS FLATBREADS AND SOUPS FROM AROUND THE WORLD

Pita

"Pita bread, the puffed pocket bread of the Middle East, is the 'go-to' bread at my house. I make it more often than pretty much anything, especially in the summer (see outdoor grill methods, page 53). It doesn't require any rest time, and as we always say in our bread classes, it is inexplicably the most fragrant bread we make. It's perfect for school lunches, and I bake it most days before my kids come downstairs in the morning. Sometimes the aroma is too enticing and it ends up being breakfast as well as lunch. Unlike loaf breads, which need to cool before eating, you can savor pita when it's still warm."—Jeff

A wide range of doughs can be used to make standard Middle Eastern pita and variations, including Greek, Italian, French, and Turkish flatbreads. Brush with water and top with seeds to add nutrition, crunch, and eye appeal.

Makes 1 pita

$^{1}/_{2}$ pound (orange-size portion) lean dough (pages 59–95)
Optional seeds: sesame, caraway, raw sunflower, poppy, flaxseed, or anise, or any
   combination you enjoy

1. **Preheat a baking stone near the middle of the oven to 500°F,** for at
    least 30 minutes.

2. Just before baking, dust the surface of the refrigerated dough with
    flour and cut off a $^{1}/_{2}$-pound (orange-size) piece. Dust the piece with
    more flour and quickly shape it into a ball by stretching the surface of
    the dough around to the bottom on all four sides, rotating the ball a
    quarter-turn as you go.

3. **Flatten the dough** with your hands and/or a
    rolling pin on a work surface, or directly onto a
    wooden pizza peel, to produce a $^{1}/_{8}$-inch-thick
    round. Dust with flour to keep the dough from
    adhering to the surface. Use a dough scraper to
    unstick the dough as needed, and transfer to a
    pizza peel if you haven't already stretched the
    dough on one. When you're finished, the dough
    round should have enough flour under it to
    move easily when you shake the peel.

4. **Slide the pita directly onto the preheated stone**—no resting time is
    needed—and bake for about 5 to 7 minutes, until very lightly
    browned and puffed. You may need to transfer the pita to a higher
    rack (without the stone) to achieve the desired degree of browning.

Don't overbake pitas (especially whole grain ones); you're going for a soft and moist result.

5. For the most authentic, soft-crusted result, wrap the flatbreads in clean cotton dish towels and set on a cooling rack when baking is complete. The pitas will deflate slightly as they cool. The space between the crusts will still be there, but may have to be nudged apart with a fork.

6. Once the pitas are cool, store in plastic bags. Pita is not harmed by airtight storage—and pitas exposed to the air become hard and stale quickly.

VARIATION: Pita with Seeds or Za'atar

Just before sliding the pitas into the oven, brush with water and sprinkle with seeds or, for an exotic Middle Eastern effect, *za'atar* spice. Caraway seeds will create a fantastic approximation of deli rye bread if you use a rye dough for this recipe (page 93 or 94).

VARIATION: Greek Style

These look like classic Middle Eastern pitas, but they are *not* puffed and don't have a pocket. They're usually enriched by brushing with melted butter or oil before baking. Use to wrap around fillings or tear apart to scoop up dips. **To bake:** start with the standard pita recipe, brush with olive oil or melted butter, then dock (puncture) the dough all over with a fork to prevent puffing. Bake as usual, checking for puffing midway through baking, and poke again with the fork to deflate if any puffy spots appear.

VARIATION: Pizza Bianca

The words *pizza bianca* simply mean "white pizza" in Italian, but this variation has nothing to do with White Pizza (page 139). Pizza bianca is really just an Italian-style, oval-shaped flatbread that is docked (punctured to prevent puffing), and then brushed with oil. Baking this Roman specialty is a simple way to demonstrate that dough always prefers to be stretched in one particular direction, especially if you're **stretching without a rolling pin** (see page 42). It's a great general principle for flatbreads—if you're in a hurry, it's always quicker to stretch an oval than try to achieve a perfect circle.

As you begin to stretch or roll your dough, determine which direction is clearly easier to elongate, then "encourage" it by stretching or rolling more vigorously in that direction, and continue until you have a long oval about 6 inches across and ¼ inch thick. Dimple with your fingertips, puncture with a fork all over, and brush generously with olive oil. A light sprinkling of fresh herbs like rosemary or thyme is optional. Bake on a preheated 500°F stone for 6 to 9 minutes, until browned, poking with a fork if it begins to puff. Pizza bianca should be browner than pita, producing a firm crust. Brush it again with olive oil when slightly cooled.

VARIATION: *Fougasse*

This glorious crusty flatbread from Provence looks difficult, but it's not. Roll out a pita into a squarish oval, then make angled slits on both sides (see photos). You may need to sprinkle more flour to decrease stickiness so the slits stay open during handling. Gently spread the holes open with your fingers, then brush with olive oil. Sprinkle with thyme, if desired.

Bake as usual for pita, but consider using a sheet pan to prevent olive oil from burning on the stone. Continue baking until richly browned (about 10 minutes)—you're going for a firm crust. Serve with tapenade (see page 213).

Turkish Pita (*Pide*)

There are several styles of pita to be found in Turkey, but this one is the most unusual. It is puffed and tends not to deflate, so it's brought to the table tall and hot from the oven. The bread is soft and slightly sweet. It is made in the same way as our regular pita bread, but in this version we've used an enriched dough.

Makes one pide

$^1/_2$ pound (orange-size portion) enriched dough (pages 107 and 251) or American-Style Pizza Dough (page 78)

Thin egg wash (1 egg mixed with 2 tablespoons water)

1 teaspoon sesame seeds

1. **Thirty minutes before baking, preheat a baking stone in the oven to 500°F.**

2. **Roll out the dough as you would for Pita** (page 199), indent the dough (see sidebar), brush lightly with egg wash, and sprinkle with sesame seeds. Check for doneness in 8 to 10 minutes; the pita should be golden brown and well puffed.

PUFFING If you are having trouble getting the pita to puff into a ball you can try this trick we learned from a baker at Depot 62, a Turkish restaurant in Manchester, Vermont. Just before you slide the pita into the oven use the handle of a wooden spoon to make a grid of shallow indents on the surface of the bread (see photo). This helps to form air pockets in the dough, which then connect and create the classic puff.

Hummus (Middle Eastern Chickpea Spread) with Lemon Zest

Hummus, the nutritious dip of the Middle East, is now served all over the world. We knew that this stuff had gone mainstream when it appeared on the sandwich menu at our favorite bagel chain restaurant right here in Minneapolis years ago. The flavor of the smooth blended chickpea and tahini (sesame paste) base is brightened by fresh lemon juice, paprika, and lots of garlic (adjust it to your taste). Our version boasts a little lemon zest, which adds a tanginess that the lemon juice alone can't match. The other variation you might enjoy is roasted garlic rather than the traditional raw; either one is delicious but the roasted garlic is less pungent and is a great way to get non-garlic lovers to try this flavorful and healthful dip with their pita bread.

Makes about 3 cups dip

2 cups dried chickpeas, covered with water and soaked overnight (or substitute 3 cups canned, drained chickpeas)

Juice from 2 lemons and their zest (removed with a Microplane)

4 large garlic cloves, or to taste, coarsely chopped (variation: 4 roasted garlic cloves, see sidebar, page 114)

$1/2$ cup tahini paste

$1/2$ teaspoon kosher salt, or more to taste

Paprika for sprinkling

Olive oil for drizzling

Black olives for garnish

1. Boil the soaked chickpeas for about 2 hours, or until soft and no longer mealy. If using canned chickpeas, drain the packing liquid, but

if you're boiling your own, reserve the cooking liquid for thinning the hummus.

2. Run all ingredients through the food processor until smooth, adding the cooking liquid if needed to produce a smooth dip; use water if you are using canned chickpeas. Depending on the capacity of your machine, you may need to do this in batches.

3. Place the hummus in a serving bowl, sprinkle lightly with paprika, and drizzle with olive oil. Garnish with whole olives and serve with warm pita.

4. The hummus can be refrigerated for up to 1 week.

Roasted Eggplant Dip (Baba Ghanoush)

We both love the Middle Eastern dip baba ghanoush. With its smoky flavor of roasted eggplant balanced by tangy lemon, it's an even more savory cousin to hummus. It's fantastic with pita bread or on sandwiches, but it's incredibly versatile—try it as a pasta sauce.

Makes about 3 cups dip

4 large eggplants
Juice from 2 lemons and their zest (removed with a Microplane)
4 large garlic cloves, or to taste, coarsely chopped (variation: 4 roasted garlic cloves, see sidebar, page 114)
3/4 cup tahini paste
1/2 teaspoon kosher salt

1. Char the eggplants on a gas or charcoal grill or under the broiler, turning occasionally, until the skin is blackened all over and the flesh is soft. Set aside to cool.

2. When the eggplant has cooled, peel with a sharp knife, and scrape the skins well because that's where you'll find the most smoky and flavorful fruit. Reserve the juice that drains from the eggplants.

3. Run all ingredients through the food processor until smooth, but hold back on reserved liquid, adding only enough to produce a smooth dip. Depending on the capacity of your machine, you may need to do this in batches.

4. Serve the baba ghanoush with fresh pita or other flatbread.

5. The dip can be refrigerated for up to 1 week.

Chicago-Style Deep-Dish Pizza, page 191

Pita and Other Flatbreads, page 199

Dips for Pita and Flatbreads, pages 204–213: clockwise from top right, ajvar, baba ghanoush, hummus, tapenade, caponata, skordalia, and tzatziki (center)

Fougasse, page 202

Crisp Pita Bread Bowl, page 214

Turkish Spiced Lamb Flatbread, page 216

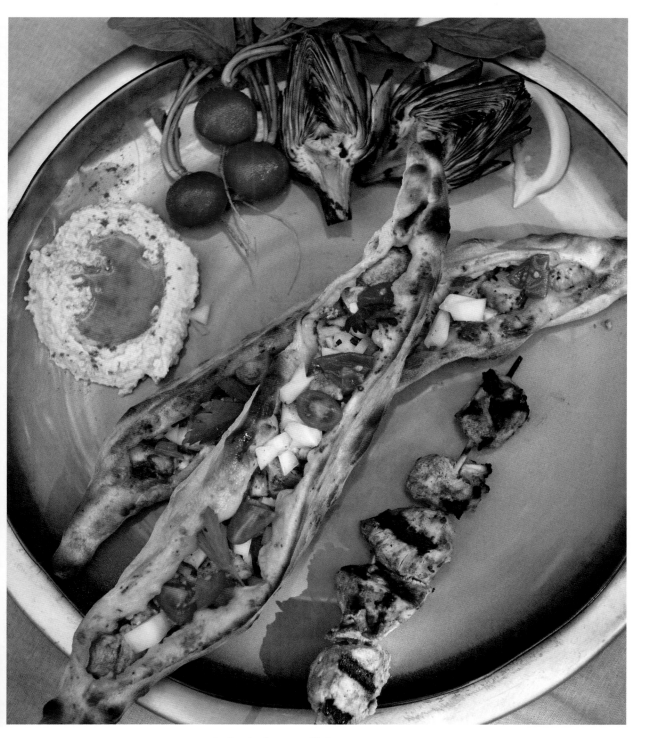

Turkish Chicken-Stuffed Pita Boats, page 219

Mexican-Style Corn Flatbread with Tomatillo, Chiles, and Queso Campesino, page 229

Brenda Langton's Curried Lentil Soup, page 227, served with Scandinavian Rye Crisps, page 234

Bing (Chinese Scallion Flatbread), page 244

Cheesy Bread Sticks, page 248

Braided Challah, page 266

Blueberry Galettes, page 269

Blush Apple Tart, page 272

Hand Pies, page 274

Skillet Peach Pie, page 279

Roasted Red Pepper and Eggplant Dip (Ajvar) from Croatia

We were wondering whether roasted red peppers and roasted eggplants might work well together. Then we heard about a blend of those flavors that's slathered onto hamburgers in Croatia—it's like no ketchup you've ever tried. *Ajvar* is also great as a dip for pita.

"Speaking of hamburgers—maybe it's just laziness, but puffed pita (pages 199 and 203) is my favorite hamburger or hot dog bun—just cut and bake the rolled-out dough in the size and shape to match your grilled meat of choice, or make a big one and break it up into hamburger-size pieces."—Jeff

Makes 1 cup dip

2 large red bell peppers

$1/2$ medium eggplant

2 large garlic cloves, or to taste, coarsely chopped (variation: 2 roasted garlic cloves, see sidebar, page 114)

$1/8$ cup olive oil

Kosher salt to taste

Freshly ground black pepper to taste

1. Roasting the peppers and eggplant: Char the peppers and eggplant under the broiler or on a gas or charcoal grill, with the skin side closest to the heat source. Turn and check often; remove from the heat when the skin has blackened, about 10 minutes. The eggplant will take longer than the peppers.

2. Drop the roasted pepper into a bowl and cover. The skin will loosen by steaming in its own heat in 10 minutes.

3. Allow the eggplant to cool, then peel by hand or with a sharp knife, scraping the skins well because that's where you'll find the most smoky and flavorful fruit. Discard the skin.

4. Gently hand-peel the pepper and discard the blackened skin; some dark bits will adhere to the pepper's flesh. Reserve the liquid that accumulates as you work with the peppers.

5. Run all ingredients and reserved liquid through a food processor until nearly smooth, adding the oil gradually. Hold back on some of the oil if the mixture is getting too thin.

6. Serve the *ajvar* with hamburgers on pita or other rolls.

7. The *ajvar* can be refrigerated for up to 1 week.

Greek, Turkish, or Indian-Style Yogurt and Cucumber Dip (*Tzatziki, Cacik, or Raita*)

This fantastic, cooling dip is perfect with Greek pita (page 199), Turkish *pide* (page 203), or Indian naan (page 222), especially when hot and spicy foods are on the menu. The Indian-style (*raita*) is pretty much the same as the Greek (*tzatziki*) and Turkish (*cacik*) varieties, but it doesn't contain garlic. Make it how you like, and consider other flavorings like paprika, lemon zest, or sesame oil.

Makes 1¼ cups dip

1 cup yogurt
½ cup shredded cucumber (use the coarse side of a box grater)
1 to 2 garlic cloves, raw or roasted (see page 114), finely minced (for Greek/ Turkish style)
1 to 2 tablespoons fresh mint leaves, finely minced
¼ teaspoon kosher salt

1. Combine all the ingredients and chill for 2 hours to allow flavors to meld.

2. Serve with pita or naan.

3. The dip can be refrigerated for up to 1 week.

Greek Garlic, Almond, and Potato Dip (*Skordalia*)

We like our potatoes unpeeled, which works well with thin-skinned potatoes like the Yukon Gold we call for here. Starchier potatoes will also work, but if the skins are thick you may prefer to peel them.

Makes 3 cups dip

5 small to medium yellow potatoes (about 1 pound), such as Yukon Gold
5 large garlic cloves, or to taste, coarsely chopped (variation: 5 roasted garlic cloves, see page 114)
$1/2$ teaspoon kosher salt
$1/2$ cup olive oil
$1/4$ cup fresh lemon juice
2 tablespoons water
$1/4$ cup almonds

1. In a large pot, cover the potatoes with cold water and bring to a boil. Cook 30 minutes until tender, drain, and set aside to cool slightly.

2. Run all ingredients through a food processor until smooth, thinning with a bit of water, if needed, until you reach dip consistency. If you prefer your almonds crunchy, add them later in the blending cycle.

3. Serve with pita or other flatbread. The *skordalia* can be refrigerated for up to 1 week.

Caponata (Sicilian Vegetable Side Dish)

Caponata is chunky enough to be served as a side dish. You can serve it warm that way, or cold with flatbread. It's related to the French *ratatouille*, but the Sicilians don't use zucchini—the bolder flavors of tomato, eggplant, garlic, and basil shine through in this dish.

Makes 3 cups dip

$^1/_2$ cup olive oil

3 medium onions, coarsely chopped

3 to 4 large garlic cloves, minced (can substitute roasted garlic, see sidebar, page 114)

2 medium unpeeled eggplants, cut into $^1/_2$-inch dice

2 celery stalks, cut into $^1/_2$-inch dice

One 28-ounce can diced tomatoes

$^1/_3$ cup wine or white vinegar

2 tablespoons sugar or honey

$^1/_4$ teaspoon hot red pepper flakes

10 fresh basil leaves, chopped or torn

$^1/_2$ cup (about $2^1/_4$ ounces) pitted and halved Mediterranean black or green olives (or use a mixture)

$^1/_4$ cup capers, drained

$^1/_4$ cup (about $1^3/_8$ ounces) pine nuts

$^1/_2$ teaspoon kosher salt

Freshly ground black pepper to taste

1. In a roomy skillet or large saucepan or pot, sauté the onions in the olive oil over medium heat until they begin to brown (you may need

to sauté in batches if your skillet isn't large enough). Add the garlic and eggplant and continue cooking until soft but not mushy. Add the celery and sauté briefly.

2. Add tomatoes, vinegar, sugar, and red pepper flakes. Bring to a simmer, and cook until the flavors meld but vegetables retain their shape. The celery should stay crunchy.

3. Remove from heat and add the basil, olives, capers, pine nuts, salt, and pepper. Taste and adjust seasonings. Serve hot or cold. The caponata stores well in the refrigerator for up to 1 week.

French Olive Spread (Tapenade)

Our tour of dips for pita and flatbread seems like a tour of the Mediterranean, and what better place to end than in the south of France, where this tapenade is a perennial favorite. The briny flavors of the anchovy are mellowed by the olives and the oil. You can even use this as a baked flatbread topping—spread it sparingly on a docked (punctured) pita before it's baked and you have a terrific hot hors d'oeuvre.

Makes 1½ cups dip

½ pound pitted black Mediterranean-style olives
4 teaspoons capers, drained
4 anchovy fillets
1 garlic clove, finely minced
¼ teaspoon dried thyme
¼ cup olive oil

1. Coarsely chop all ingredients together in a food processor and serve with *fougasse* (page 202), or any flatbread you like.

2. Tapenade stores in the refrigerator for up to 1 week.

Visit PizzaIn5.com, where you'll find recipes, photos, videos, and instructional material. See page 53 for outdoor grill instructions.

Crisp Pita Bread Bowl

A paper-thin pita is baked until it puffs and then becomes crisp. We break into the top and fill it with a delicate green salad. It is quick, delicious, and elegant.

Makes 2 pita bowls

$^{1}/_{2}$ pound (orange-size portion) lean dough (pages 59–95)
Flour for the pizza peel

1. **Preheat a baking stone for 30 minutes to 500°F.** Sprinkle a pizza peel liberally with flour. Dust the surface of the refrigerated dough with flour and cut off a $^{1}/_{2}$-pound (orange-size) piece. Dust with more flour and quickly shape it into a ball by stretching the surface of the dough around to the bottom on all four sides, rotating the ball a quarter-turn as you go. Divide the dough into two equal pieces and form them into balls.

2. **Stretch the pita:** Flatten the dough with your hands and/or a rolling pin on a work surface, or directly onto a wooden pizza peel, to produce a $^{1}/_{16}$-inch-thick round (about 8 inches in diameter). Dust with flour to keep the dough from adhering to the surface. Use a dough scraper to unstick the dough as needed, and transfer to a pizza peel if you haven't already stretched the dough on one. (See Tips and Techniques, page 47, if you'd rather bake on a sheet pan.) When you're finished, the dough rounds should have enough flour under them to move easily when you shake the peel.

3. **Slide the pitas onto the preheated stone** (see Step 11, page 67):
    Check for doneness in 10 minutes; at this time, turn the pitas around
    in the oven if one side is browning faster than the other. It may take
    up to 5 minutes more in the oven for the pitas to be golden brown
    and crisp.

4. Allow to cool completely, preferably on a wire cooling rack. To serve,
    break open a 3-inch hole in the top of the crisp pitas and fill with
    your favorite green salad.

Visit PizzaIn5.com, where you'll find recipes, photos, videos, and instructional material. See
page 53 for outdoor grill instructions.

Turkish Spiced Lamb Flatbread (*Lahmacun*)

"My friend Serap is a native of Istanbul and now owns Depot 62, a Turkish restaurant in Manchester, Vermont. She introduced my family to this richly spiced lamb-covered flatbread. When it came to the table, she sprinkled it with fresh parsley, squeezed a lemon over the top, and then rolled it up like a crepe. Of all the delicious foods she presented to us this was the most loved."—Zoë

Makes one 10-inch flatbread (makes enough lamb for 4 flatbreads)

$1/4$ pound (peach-size portion) lean or gluten-free dough from pages 59–98

2 tablespoons olive oil

$1/2$ yellow or white onion, finely chopped

$1^1/2$ teaspoons ground cumin

$1^1/2$ teaspoons ground coriander

1 teaspoon paprika

1 pound ground lamb

1 tablespoon tomato paste

1 teaspoon salt

2 tablespoons finely chopped flat-leaf parsley

Flour for the pizza peel

Toppings

$1/4$ cup flat-leaf parsley

$1/4$ cup chopped yellow or white onions

$1/4$ cup chopped tomatoes

1 lemon, cut in quarters

1. **Prepare the spicy lamb:** Place a skillet over medium heat and add the olive oil and chopped onion. Cook, stirring, until the onion is soft but not brown. Add the spices and cook for a minute, then add the ground lamb. Cook the lamb until it is evenly browned, breaking it up as it browns. Stir in the tomato paste, salt, and parsley. Set aside to cool before topping the flatbread. The lamb can be made in advance and stored in the refrigerator for 3 days.

2. **Preheat a baking stone to 500°F for at least 30 minutes.** Sprinkle a pizza peel liberally with flour. Dust the surface of the refrigerated dough with flour and cut off a ¼-pound (peach-size) piece. Dust with more flour and quickly shape it into a ball by stretching the surface of the dough around to the bottom on all four sides, rotating the ball a quarter-turn as you go.

3. **Stretch the flatbread:** Flatten the dough with your hands and/or a rolling pin on a work surface, or directly onto the wooden pizza peel, to produce a 1/16-inch-thick round (about 10 inches across). Dust with flour to keep the dough from adhering to the surface. Use a dough scraper to unstick the dough as needed, and transfer to a pizza peel if you haven't already stretched the dough on one. (See Tips and Techniques, page 47, if you'd rather bake on a sheet pan.) When you're finished, the dough round should have enough flour under it to move easily when you shake the peel.

4. **Add the meat:** Spread ⅓ cup of the meat evenly over the disk of dough. Save the remaining meat for more pizzas or freeze.

5. **Slide the flatbread onto the preheated stone** (see Step 11, page 67): If you're using a sheet pan, place it right on the stone. Check for

Visit PizzaIn5.com, where you'll find recipes, photos, videos, and instructional material. See page 53 for outdoor grill instructions.

doneness in 5 to 8 minutes, the crust should be baked through but remain pale and soft.

6. Serve immediately with chopped parsley, onions, tomatoes, and a squeeze of fresh lemon. Cut into slices or roll up the flatbread like a crepe and enjoy!

Turkish Chicken-Stuffed Pita Boats

This pita is stuffed with marinated grilled chicken and formed in the shape of a canoe. In Istanbul they are served everywhere—just as ubiquitous as a slice of pizza in New York City. They can be filled with chicken, spicy lamb (page 216), or even pepperoni. This pita makes a great meal to eat on the run.

Makes four 12-inch-long pita boats

1 pound (grapefruit-size portion) lean dough (pages 59–95)
Flour, cornmeal, or parchment paper for the pizza peel

Chicken and Marinade
1 cup (8 ounces) plain yogurt (whole milk or nonfat)
1 teaspoon hot red pepper flakes
$1/4$ teaspoon cayenne pepper
1 teaspoon sweet paprika
2 tablespoons olive oil
2 tablespoons red wine vinegar
1 tablespoon tomato paste
2 teaspoons kosher salt
1 teaspoon freshly ground black pepper
2 garlic cloves, finely minced
Juice and chopped peel of $1/2$ lemon
1 pound boneless chicken thighs, cut into 1-inch cubes

Kebabs
2 large green bell peppers, cored, seeded, cut into 8 pieces
2 sweet white onions, peeled, cut in quarters

Visit PizzaIn5.com, where you'll find recipes, photos, videos, and instructional material. See page 53 for outdoor grill instructions.

1 lemon, cut in quarters for grilling

2 tablespoons olive oil

Salt and freshly ground black pepper

4 skewers

1 cup crumbled feta cheese

1 cup Greek, Turkish, or Indian Style Yogurt and Cucumber Dip (see page 209)

1. **Marinate the chicken:** Combine the ingredients for the marinade in a large bowl. Mix in the cubed chicken, cover, and allow to sit in the refrigerator for at least 2 hours, or overnight.

2. **Prepare the kebabs:** Preheat a grill to medium-high heat, and brush the grates with oil. Alternate pieces of chicken, bell peppers, and onions on the skewers, ending with a lemon wedge. Brush the vegetables with olive oil and sprinkle with salt and pepper. Grill until the chicken is just cooked through, 10 to 15 minutes, turning to sear the meat on all sides. Allow the skewers to cool slightly, remove the chicken and vegetables from the skewers, and coarsely chop, leaving the lemons intact for serving on the side.

3. **Preheat a baking stone to 500°F for at least 30 minutes.** Dust the surface of the refrigerated dough with flour and cut off a 1-pound (grapefruit-size) piece. Dust with more flour and quickly shape it into a ball by stretching the surface of the dough around to the bottom on all four sides, rotating the ball a quarter-turn as you go. Divide the ball into 4 equal pieces and form them into balls, using more flour to prevent sticking.

4. **Stretch the pita:** Flatten the dough with your hands and a rolling pin on a work surface, or directly onto the wooden pizza peel (or shape

the disk by hand, see page 42), to produce a $^1/_{16}$-inch-thick oval (12 inches long and 4 inches wide). Dust with flour to keep the dough from adhering to the surface. Use a dough scraper to unstick the dough as needed, and transfer to a pizza peel if you haven't already stretched the dough on one. (See page 47 if you'd rather bake on a sheet pan.) When you're finished, the dough should have enough flour under it to move easily when you shake the peel.

5. **Add the filling:** Spread the chopped meat and vegetables and the feta over the center of the dough, leaving a $^1/_2$-inch border of dough around it. Starting with the long side, fold the dough up over the filling; the dough will come halfway into the middle. Fold the other side over to form a canoe shape. Pinch the overlapping ends together to make a good seal, and press the sides down to seal the edges. Position the pita on the peel so the pointed end will slide onto the stone. Repeat with the other flatbreads. (If your stone will only hold two flatbreads at a time, wait to roll and fill the other two until just before baking.)

6. **Slide the pita (pointed end first) onto the preheated stone** (see Step 11, page 67): If you're using a sheet pan, place it directly on the stone. Check for doneness in 8 to 10 minutes and turn the flatbread around in the oven if one side is browning faster than the other.

7. Allow to cool slightly, preferably on a wire cooling rack. Serve with the grilled lemon wedges and yogurt-mint sauce.

Visit PizzaIn5.com, where you'll find recipes, photos, videos, and instructional material. See page 53 for outdoor grill instructions.

Baked Naan

In our first book, *Artisan Bread in Five Minutes a Day*, we made a stovetop version of this wonderful bread. It was cooked, rather than baked, in a hot skillet with ghee—quite untraditional and yet absolutely delicious. This version is just as quick and easy, but we have you quickly baking the dough on a hot stone in the oven and then slathering the bread with melted ghee. The result is a bit more traditional and equally delicious. We have developed a naan dough made with yogurt to give the flatbread even more depth of flavor, but this recipe can be made with any of the yeasted doughs in chapters 5 or 6, *except* for the *injera* dough. This bread is wonderful served with soups, stews, curries, and the yogurt-based dips on page 209.

Makes one 12-inch naan

$^1/_2$ pound (orange-size portion) naan dough (page 88), or any lean or gluten-free
    dough from pages 59–98
Flour for the pizza peel

Topping
Melted ghee or butter to brush on top of the baked naan
Salt to taste

1. **Preheat a baking stone at your oven's highest temperature for at least 30 minutes.** Sprinkle a pizza peel liberally with flour. Dust the surface of the refrigerated dough with flour and cut off a $^1/_2$-pound (orange-size) piece. Dust with more flour and quickly shape it into a ball by stretching the surface of the dough around to the bottom on all four sides, rotating the ball a quarter-turn as you go.

2. **Roll out and stretch the naan:** Flatten the dough with your hands and/ or a rolling pin on a work surface, or directly onto a wooden pizza peel, to produce a $\frac{1}{8}$-inch-thick round. Dust with flour to keep the dough from adhering to the surface. Use a dough scraper to unstick the dough as needed, and transfer to a pizza peel if you haven't already stretched the dough on one. (See page 47 if you'd rather bake on a sheet pan.) When you're finished, the dough should have enough flour under it to move easily when you shake the peel. Poke several holes in the dough with a fork to prevent it from puffing in the oven.

3. **Slide the naan onto the preheated stone** (see Step 11, page 67): If you're using a sheet pan, place it right on the stone. Check for doneness in 5 minutes and turn the naan around in the oven if one side is browning faster than the other.

4. Slather the hot naan with the melted ghee, sprinkle with salt, and tear off pieces to serve.

VARIATION: Garlic Naan

Just before sliding the dough into the oven, brush with melted ghee, press 1 tablespoon minced garlic into the surface of the dough and sprinkle with salt. No need to slather with more ghee after baking.

Stuffed Naan

"My favorite part of going out for Indian food is the fresh, hot, stuffed naan they pull from the tandoor oven. Chewy, soft dough wrapped around fragrant fillings and infused with the smokiness of the blazing hot oven is fantastic on its own, or dipped into hot curries.

"One night, at my favorite Indian restaurant, I asked our server if I could watch the chef in action and was delighted to be led to the kitchen. The speed, grace, and fearlessness with which he created these breads was awe-inspiring. The following technique is what he taught me. We don't have a tandoor oven so we bake it on a stone."—Zoë

Makes 1 stuffed naan

¹/₂ pound (orange-size portion) naan dough (page 88) or any lean dough (pages 59–95)
Flour or parchment paper for the pizza peel

Stuffing
3 tablespoons finely chopped white onion
3 tablespoons finely chopped cilantro
Salt to taste
Melted ghee or butter to brush on top of the baked naan

1. **Preheat a baking stone at your oven's highest temperature for at least 30 minutes.** Sprinkle a pizza peel liberally with flour. Dust the surface of the refrigerated dough with flour and cut off a ¹/₂-pound (orange-size) piece. Dust with more flour and quickly shape it into a

ball by stretching the surface of the dough around to the bottom on all four sides, rotating the ball a quarter-turn as you go.

2. **Stretch the naan:** Flatten the dough with your hands and/or a rolling pin on a work surface, or directly onto a wooden pizza peel, to produce a ¼-inch-thick round. Dust with flour to keep the dough from adhering to the surface. Use a dough scraper to unstick the dough as needed, and transfer to a pizza peel if you haven't already stretched the dough on one. (See page 47 if you'd rather bake on a sheet pan.) When you're finished, the dough should have enough flour under it to move easily when you shake the peel.

3. **Add the stuffing:** Spread the onions, cilantro, and salt over the dough, then pinch the edges shut around it like a purse, to form a ball around the stuffing. Roll the dough out again to a ⅛-inch-thick oval. Be sure to add enough flour to keep it from sticking.

4. **Slide the stuffed naan onto the preheated stone** (see Step 11, page 67): If you're using a sheet pan, place it right on the stone. Check for doneness in 8 to 10 minutes and turn the naan around in the oven if one side is browning faster than the other.

5. Immediately brush with ghee and tear off pieces to serve.

VARIATIONS
Replace the stuffing with either of the following:

Chickpea and Garlic

1 tablespoon minced garlic

$1/4$ cup finely chopped cooked or canned chickpeas

Pinch salt

Cauliflower

1 tablespoon curry powder or paste

$1/4$ cup very finely chopped cooked cauliflower

Pinch salt

Brenda Langton's Curried Lentil Soup

"A friend brought a terrific curried lentil soup to the hospital when our second child was born, and it was the silkiest lentil soup I'd ever tasted. Coconut milk and sweet potato smooth out the texture of lentils, and the chili pepper makes it quite addictive—so I asked for the recipe. It turned out that the source was Brenda Langton—the vegetarian recipes from her fantastic restaurants, Cafe Brenda and now, Spoonriver, show that going without meat doesn't mean going without flavor and beautiful presentation. This recipe is adapted from The Cafe Brenda Cookbook.*"—Jeff*

Serves 6 to 8

2 tablespoons neutral-flavored oil

1 large onion, diced

$1/4$ cup peeled and minced fresh ginger

6 large garlic cloves, minced

$1^1/2$ tablespoons curry powder

$1/4$ teaspoon hot red pepper flakes, or to taste

4 medium carrots, scraped and diced

1 medium sweet red bell pepper, cored, seeded, and diced

5 cups diced, unpeeled sweet potato (about $1^1/2$ pounds)

One 14-ounce can coconut milk (regular or "light")

2 cups dried lentils, picked over and washed

8 cups water, vegetable stock, or chicken stock

2 teaspoons salt (decrease if using salty stock)

Juice of $1/2$ lime, or more to taste

1 bunch cilantro, tough stems removed, minced

$1/2$ teaspoon orange zest (optional)

Visit PizzaIn5.com, where you'll find recipes, photos, videos, and instructional material. See page 53 for outdoor grill instructions.

1. In a 6-quart saucepan, sauté the onion and ginger in the oil until wilted and fragrant. Add the garlic, curry powder, red pepper flakes, carrots, bell pepper, and sweet potatoes and sauté briefly.

2. Add the coconut milk, lentils, water or stock, and salt. Simmer, partly covered, until lentils and sweet potatoes are tender, about 45 minutes.

3. For a smooth soup, cool and run through the food processor, or use an immersion blender right in the pot. Add lime juice, cilantro, and orange zest, if using, just before serving.

Mexican-Style Corn Flatbread with Tomatillo, Chiles, and *Queso Campesino*

Mexico has a wonderful wheat bread tradition, which usually rests in the shadow of its corn masa, usually used for tortillas (see page 103). We decided to marry the two in this south-of-the-border inspired snack. Tomatillos are sometimes called Mexican green tomatoes. They have a tartness you don't find in regular tomatoes and they really make this flatbread special (though ordinary tomatoes or tomato sauce can be substituted here). We call for fresh Mexican crumbling cheese—if you can't get *queso campesino* or *queso fresco* for crumbling where you live, other kinds of crumbly farmer cheese (or even mozzarella) work well in the recipe. And if you like things hot and spicy, use the jalapeños or serranos, or pass them at the table, along with Mexican hot sauce. Red serranos make a particularly beautiful feast for the eyes.

Makes one 12-inch pizza flatbread

$^1/_2$ pound (orange-size portion) corn masa (page 90), or other lean dough (pages 59–95)

$^1/_3$ cup Tomatillo Sauce (see page 119)

3 ounces *queso campesino* or *queso fresco* for crumbling

$^1/_4$ jalapeño or red serrano pepper, finely minced (optional and to taste)

Flour, cornmeal, or parchment paper for the pizza peel

Kosher salt to taste

1. **Prepare and measure** all toppings in advance.

2. **Preheat a baking stone at your oven's highest temperature for at least 30 minutes.** Sprinkle a pizza peel liberally with flour. Dust the

surface of the refrigerated dough with flour and cut off a $1/2$-pound (orange-size) piece. Dust with more flour and quickly shape it into a ball by stretching the surface of the dough around to the bottom on all four sides, rotating the ball a quarter-turn as you go.

3. **Stretch the crust:** Flatten the dough with your hands and/or a rolling pin on a work surface, or directly onto the wooden pizza peel, to produce a $1/8$-inch-thick round. Dust with flour to keep the dough from adhering to the surface. Use a dough scraper to unstick the dough as needed, and transfer to a pizza peel if you haven't already stretched the dough on one. (See page 47 if you'd rather bake on a sheet pan.) When you're finished, the dough round should have enough flour under it to move easily when you shake the peel.

4. **Add the toppings:** Spread the tomatillo sauce over the dough, then add the cheese. Finish with jalapeños or serrano chiles, if you're using chiles.

5. **Slide the flatbread onto the preheated stone** (See Step 11, page 67): If you're using a sheet pan, place it right on the stone. Check for doneness in 8 to 10 minutes and turn the flatbread around in the oven if one side is browning faster than the other.

6. Sprinkle with coarse salt to taste and allow to cool slightly, preferably on a wire cooling rack. Cut into wedges and serve with additional minced hot chiles and Mexican hot sauce if desired.

Cuban Black Bean Soup (and a Mexican Pinto Bean Variation)

In Latin American cooking, there's an old saw that goes something like this: pinto beans (the pink ones) are from the interior of Mexico and Central America, and black beans are Caribbean—used on the Yucatan coast and on the islands. Cuba's famous black bean soup is the epitome of simple black bean cuisine. Its savory clean flavor is nicely accented by the sharp rice garnish—it isn't traditional to use hot chiles in this kind of soup.

The Mexican-style variation trades the rice-and-vinegar garnish for the heat of chile peppers. You can ramp up the heat however you like using Mexican hot sauce. With both of these terrific soups, you can serve any flatbread you like for dipping, but we think the Mexican-Style Corn Flatbread (page 229) or corn tortillas (page 103) are particularly nice.

Serves 8

Rice Garnish
1 cup cooked white or brown rice
$1/8$ cup finely chopped onion
$1/8$ cup vinegar (white, cider, or wine)
1 tablespoon olive oil

Soup
$1/4$ cup olive oil
2 medium yellow or white onions, chopped
1 red bell pepper, cored, seeded, and diced
3 large garlic cloves, finely chopped
1 tablespoon ground cumin

1 teaspoon dried oregano (or 3 teaspoons chopped fresh oregano)

Soaking liquid: 2 quarts water, chicken broth, beef broth, or vegetable broth

3 cups black beans, rinsed and picked over to remove debris and soaked in water or broth overnight in a roomy soup pot (or substitute five 15-ounce cans plus $2/3$ cup water or broth)

$1/8$ cup vinegar (white, cider, or wine)

1 teaspoon salt or more to taste

Freshly ground black pepper to taste

Optional Toppings: yogurt, sour cream, or *crema fresca*, and/or roasted red pepper, slivered (see pages 207–208)

1. **Prepare the rice garnish:** Mix the rice with the onion, vinegar, and oil and set aside.

2. **Prepare the soup:** Sauté the onions and pepper in the olive oil over medium heat in a heavy 5-quart soup pot until they begin to brown. Add the garlic, cumin, and oregano and continue sautéing until fragrant, then add the dried soaked beans and their soaking liquid (or the canned beans and $2/3$ cup water or broth).

3. Add the vinegar, bring to a simmer, and cook until the beans are tender, 1 to 3 hours, depending on the age of your dried beans. Add water if needed, to keep the beans covered. If using canned beans, only a 20- to 30-minute simmer is needed.

4. Add salt and pepper to taste—dried beans will need more salt than canned.

5. Serve with a dollop of the rice garnish, and if desired, a spoonful of yogurt, sour cream, or *crema fresca*, and slivered roasted red pepper. The soup freezes well.

VARIATION: Mexican Pinto Bean

Substitute pinto beans for the black beans, and add 1 seeded and ground dried New Mexico Red or *guajillo* pepper in Step 2 (use a coffee grinder). Omit the vinegar from the soup and skip the rice garnish entirely. Pass Mexican hot sauce at the table and serve with yogurt, sour cream, or *crema fresca*, and Mexican-Style Corn Flatbread (page 229).

Visit PizzaIn5.com, where you'll find recipes, photos, videos, and instructional material. See page 53 for outdoor grill instructions.

Scandinavian Rye Crisps (*Knekkebrød*), Lavash, and Other Crackers

In Norway, rye crackers are called *knekkebrød (knék-eh-bro)*, which basically means "crackly bread." They're superhealthy, crunchy, and cannot miss when topped with traditional *gietost (yi-toast)*—a Norwegian brown cheese made from scalded milk—or smoked fish with capers (or try them with more readily available Norwegian Jarlsberg, or smoked gouda). We bake them at a low temperature to dry them out for storage rather than trying to brown them very much, which can produce a scorched flavor. **If you make crackers from other lean doughs**, you have something closer to the cracker-crisp version of the Central Asian *lavash*, especially with sesame seeds. Vary the doughs and toppings to create any kind of cracker that you enjoy. We like these made as large sheets, but you can cut them up with a pizza wheel and bake as small crackers.

Makes 2 or more thin crisps, depending on size

¼-pound (peach-size portion) Rustic and Hearty Rye (page 93), *Knekkebrød* dough (page 94), or other lean dough (pages 59–95)

Oil for brushing (optional)

Seed mixture for sprinkling: sesame, flaxseed, caraway, raw sunflower, poppy seed, and/or aniseed (optional)

Coarse salt for sprinkling (optional)

Oil or parchment paper for the baking sheet

1. **Preheat the oven to 350°F.** Oil a baking sheet or line with parchment paper. Dust the surface of the refrigerated dough with flour and break off a ¼-pound (peach-size) piece. The dough will have little

resiliency or stretch so you won't be able to shape it in the usual way—just pat it into a ball, using as much flour as needed so it can be handled.

2. **Roll out the *knekkebrød*:** Flatten the dough with your hands and/or a rolling pin on a flour-dusted work surface to produce a $1/16$-inch-thick round; divide it into smaller balls if you're having a hard time with the larger piece. Dust with flour to keep the dough from adhering to the surface. Use a dough scraper to unstick the dough as needed, and transfer to the prepared baking sheet. Another way to achieve this thickness is to use the rolling instructions for the gluten-free dough (page 104).

3. Brush the dough with oil and/or seeds if desired. If using seeds but not oil, brush with water before sprinkling on the seeds. Sprinkle with salt if desired.

4. **Place the baking sheet** in the oven and bake for about 25 minutes; you will see some light browning but don't overdo it or you'll get a scorched flavor. Fully baked *knekkebrød* should be firm but won't crisp until cool.

Visit PizzaIn5.com, where you'll find recipes, photos, videos, and instructional material. See page 53 for outdoor grill instructions.

Scandinavian Smoked Salmon Flatbread with Capers and Dill

Cream cheese with smoked salmon on bagels is often considered to be purely American—mainly because cream cheese is an American invention. Here's a little homage to those flavors, done Scandinavian-style on a rye base with capers and dill. Remember that the salmon isn't baked with the pizza, and use the red onion for a little extra zing if you like.

Makes one 12-inch flatbread

$^1/_2$-pound (orange-size portion) Rustic and Hearty Rye (page 93), *Knekkebrød* dough (page 94), or other lean or gluten-free dough (page 59–98)

3 ounces Jarlsberg or Swiss cheese, sliced thinly

4 ounces sliced smoked salmon

2 teaspoons fresh chopped dill

1 teaspoon capers, drained

1 teaspoon minced red onion (optional)

Flour, cornmeal, parchment paper, or rice flour for the pizza peel

1. **Preheat a baking stone at your oven's highest temperature for at least 30 minutes** (see "Why Such a Short Preheat," page 49). Sprinkle a pizza peel liberally with flour. Dust the surface of the refrigerated dough with flour and cut off a $^1/_2$-pound (orange-size) piece. Dust with more flour and quickly shape it into a ball by stretching the surface of the dough around to the bottom on all four sides, rotating the ball a quarter-turn as you go.

2. **Stretch the flatbread crust:** Flatten the dough with your hands and/or a rolling pin on a work surface, or directly onto a wooden pizza peel,

to produce a ¹/₈-inch-thick round. Dust with flour to keep the dough from adhering to the surface. Use a dough scraper to unstick the dough as needed, and transfer to a pizza peel if you haven't already stretched the dough on one. (See page 47 if you'd rather bake on a sheet pan.) When you're finished, the dough round should have enough flour under it to move easily when you shake the peel.

3. Distribute the cheese slices over the dough.

4. **Slide the flatbread onto the preheated stone** (see Step 11, page 67): If you're using a baking sheet, place it right on the stone. Check for doneness in 8 to 10 minutes and turn the flatbread around in the oven if one side is browning faster than the other.

5. Immediately distribute the salmon, dill, capers, and onions, if using, over the cheese. Cut into wedges and serve.

Visit PizzaIn5.com, where you'll find recipes, photos, videos, and instructional material. See page 53 for outdoor grill instructions.

Scandinavian Fish Soup with Dill, Snipped Chives, and Potato

This is an extremely simple soup inspired by the flavors of Scandinavia. Dill and potato are mild and comforting. The traditional choice would be cod, but any firm, non-oily white fish (or a combination) works well in the recipe.

Serves 8

3 tablespoons butter or vegetable oil

1 medium onion, chopped

2 shallots, chopped

3 tablespoons minced fresh dill, or $1^1/_2$ tablespoons dried

4 cups fish stock or water, (or two 8-ounce bottles of clam juice plus 2 cups water)

4 medium potatoes (peeled or unpeeled), cut into $^1/_2$-inch dice (about 1 pound)

1 bay leaf

$^1/_8$ teaspoon saffron threads

2 teaspoons kosher salt (decrease to taste)

Freshly ground black pepper to taste

3 pounds white, non-oily boneless fish

One recipe Béchamel Sauce (page 117), or 2 cups cream

2 tablespoons snipped fresh chives

1. In a large stockpot, sauté the onions and shallots over medium heat in butter or oil until they begin to brown. Add the dill and continue to cook until aromatic.

2. Add the fish stock or water (or water/clam juice), potatoes, bay leaf, saffron threads, salt, and pepper and bring to a boil. Cover, lower the heat, and simmer for 30 minutes, or until potatoes are tender.

3. Cut the fish into bite-size portions and bring the soup back to a rapid boil. Add fish and cook for 1 minute.

4. Add the béchamel sauce or cream and gently heat through; don't bring to a simmer or it may curdle.

5. Add the chives just before serving hot, with Scandinavian Rye Crisps (page 234).

Gluten-Free Spicy Garlic Beef Pizza

This pizza sizzles with flavorful garlic, coconut milk, and hot sauce. We like the topping kicked up with spice and finished off with a cooling squeeze of lime.

Makes one 12-inch pizza

$1/2$ pound (orange-size portion) Gluten-Free Pizza and Flatbread Dough (page 96)
$1/4$ cup hoisin sauce
1 cup Spicy Garlic Beef (page 242)
2 tablespoons chopped scallions
2 tablespoons chopped cilantro
2 tablespoons chopped dry-roasted peanuts (can substitute your favorite nuts)
Wedge of lime
Rice flour or parchment paper for the pizza peel (see sidebar, page 104)

1. **Prepare and measure** all toppings in advance.

2. **Preheat a baking stone at your oven's highest temperature for at least 30 minutes** (see "Why Such a Short Preheat," page 49). Sprinkle a pizza peel liberally with rice flour. Dust the surface of the refrigerated dough with rice flour and cut off a $1/2$-pound (orange-size) piece. Dust the piece with more flour and quickly shape it into a ball; this dough isn't stretched because there is no gluten in it—just gently press it into the shape of a ball. You will need to use lots of rice flour to prevent the dough from sticking to your hands and the work surface, but avoid working lumps of flour into the dough.

3. **Flatten the dough** with your hands and a rolling pin directly onto a pizza peel to produce a $\frac{1}{8}$-inch-thick round. Dust with quite a bit of rice flour to keep the dough from adhering to the surface. Use a dough scraper to unstick the dough as needed, and transfer to a pizza peel if you haven't already stretched the dough on one. (See page 104 for more tips on working with gluten-free dough.) When you're finished, the dough round should have enough flour under it to move easily when you shake the peel.

4. **Add the toppings:** Spread the hoisin sauce over the dough, then add the spicy beef.

5. **Slide the pizza onto the preheated stone** (see Step 11, page 67): If you're using a sheet pan, place it right on the stone. Check for doneness in 8 to 10 minutes and turn the pizza around in the oven if one side is browning faster than the other. If the bottom crust is not browning, see page 48.

6. Allow to cool slightly, preferably on a wire cooling rack. Evenly sprinkle the pizza with chopped scallions, cilantro, and peanuts, and then squeeze the lime over the top. Cut into wedges and serve.

Visit PizzaIn5.com, where you'll find recipes, photos, videos, and instructional material. See page 53 for outdoor grill instructions.

Spicy Garlic Beef

Some like it hot—we do!—but feel free to tone down the spices. This recipe is excellent mild, too, and either way, the fresh cilantro and lime provide a great contrast. Swap in chicken, pork, or tofu if that tickles your fancy.

Makes enough to top two 12-inch pizzas

1 pound sirloin or flank steak, cut into thin slices (see sidebar), or use chicken, pork, or tofu

$1/2$ teaspoon salt

$1/2$ teaspoon freshly ground black pepper

2 tablespoons sesame or peanut oil

2 garlic cloves, peeled and finely minced

One-inch piece fresh ginger, peeled and finely minced

2 tablespoons finely chopped scallions

1 teaspoon Sriracha sauce, or more to taste

$1/2$ cup rice wine vinegar

2 tablespoons sugar

$1/2$ cup unsweetened coconut milk

∾

The easiest way to cut meat thin, as we require for the beef in this recipe, about $1/16$ inch thick, is to freeze it for 10 minutes—just long enough to make the outer layer of the meat is stiff enough to slice evenly.

1. Pat the meat dry and sprinkle with the salt and pepper. In a large skillet, heat the oil over medium-high heat, being careful not to let it smoke. Add the beef and brown on both sides, about 2 minutes. Reduce the heat to medium and add the garlic, ginger, scallions, Sriracha, vinegar,

and sugar. Stir on occasion and let simmer for about 15 minutes. All of the liquid will cook off and the meat will be nicely caramelized.

2. Reduce the heat to low, add the coconut milk, and continue to cook until it is thickened, about 5 minutes.

Visit PizzaIn5.com, where you'll find recipes, photos, videos, and instructional material. See page 53 for outdoor grill instructions.

Bing (Chinese Scallion Flatbread Done on the Stovetop)

"My friend Allison used to work at a university, where she met interesting people from around the world. Once she invited an exchange student from China to a party; his potluck contribution was this scrumptious oniony flatbread. Bing is the general term for Chinese flatbreads, and there are a multitude of styles. This one's done right on the stovetop so you don't need to heat up the oven. Its roll-up-and-flatten technique provides an almost-flaky texture, and the sesame oil plus raw scallion in the filling create the authentic flavor (or vary it with rendered chicken fat). Look for the sesame oil in your grocery or an Asian specialty store—you can make the filling with neutral-flavored oil but the flavor just won't be the same."—Jeff

Makes one 12-inch flatbread

$1/2$ pound (orange-size portion) lean dough (pages 59–95)

2 teaspoons sesame oil or rendered chicken fat

3 medium scallions, sliced into thin rings

$1/4$ teaspoon kosher salt

2 tablespoons peanut oil (or substitute any neutral-flavored oil with a high smoke-temperature such as canola, corn, or soybean)

1. Dust the surface of the refrigerated dough with flour and cut off a $1/2$-pound (orange-size) piece. Dust with more flour and quickly shape it into a ball by stretching the surface of the dough around to the bottom on all four sides, rotating the ball a quarter-turn as you go. Flatten with your fingers and a rolling pin to about $1/8$ inch thick.

2. Spread the sesame oil over the surface of the dough, and distribute the scallions and salt, leaving a $1/2$-inch border at the edge. Roll up into a rope, then coil the rope tightly around itself. Place it on a work surface and allow it to rest, loosely covered with plastic wrap or a bowl, for 20 minutes.

3. **Flatten the coiled dough** into an $1/8$-inch thick round and set aside. Heat a 12-inch cast-iron skillet over high heat on the stovetop, until water droplets flicked into the pan skitter across the surface and evaporate quickly. Add 2 tablespoons peanut oil, and allow to heat until hot *but not smoking.*

4. Brush off excess flour from the rolled-out dough and place it in the hot skillet. Decrease the heat to medium, and cover to trap the steam and heat.

5. Check for doneness with a spatula at 2 to 5 minutes, or sooner if you smell scorching. Adjust the heat as needed. Flip when the underside is richly browned.

6. Continue cooking another 2 to 5 minutes, until the flatbread feels firm, even at the edges, and the second side is browned. You'll need more pan time if you've rolled a thicker one.

7. Allow to cool slightly on a rack before breaking apart and eating. Serve with Asian hot pepper sauce, such as Sriracha.

Visit PizzaIn5.com, where you'll find recipes, photos, videos, and instructional material. See page 53 for outdoor grill instructions.

Sesame Spiral Flatbread

The richness of sesame seeds is combined with the fresh flavor of the *za'atar* spice mix to create this stunning bread. We love it served with hummus (page 204) or with soup (page 227). This spiral flatbread is also delicious made with tapenade or pesto (see variations below).

Makes one 10-inch flatbread

$1/2$ pound (orange-size portion) lean dough (pages 59–95)

2 tablespoons olive oil for the pie tin

2 tablespoons sesame oil

$1/4$ cup sesame seeds, toasted

4 tablespoons *za'atar* spice mix (or make your own by mixing 2 parts dried thyme, 1 part ground sumac, and 1 part sesame seeds)

$1/4$ teaspoon coarse sea salt

1. **Preheat the oven to 450°F.** Rub 2 tablespoons of the olive oil in the bottom of a pie tin, set aside. Dust the surface of the refrigerated dough with flour and cut off a $1/2$-pound (orange-size) piece. Dust with more flour and quickly shape it into a ball by stretching the surface of the dough around to the bottom on all four sides, rotating the ball a quarter-turn as you go.

2. **Stretch the dough:** Flatten the dough with your hands and/or a rolling pin on a work surface, or directly onto the wooden pizza peel, to produce a $1/8$-inch-thick round. Dust with flour to keep the dough from adhering to the surface. Use a dough scraper to unstick the dough as needed. Spread the sesame oil over the dough with a pastry

brush, then sprinkle on the sesame seeds, *za'atar*, and salt. Roll up into a rope, then coil the rope tightly around itself. Place it on a work surface and allow it to rest, loosely covered with plastic wrap, for 20 minutes. Dust with more flour and roll out the spiraled ball into a ¼-inch disk. Transfer to the prepared pie tin and allow to rest for another 15 minutes.

3. **Slide the pie plate into the oven on the middle rack:** Check for doneness in 25 minutes and turn the flatbread around in the oven if one side is browning faster than the other. It may take up to 5 minutes more in the oven.

4. Remove the flatbread from the pie tin and allow to cool slightly, preferably on a wire cooling rack. Cut into wedges and serve.

VARIATION:
Spread ½ cup tapenade (page 213) or pesto (page 114) on the dough before rolling the dough into a log. Bake as above.

Visit PizzaIn5.com, where you'll find recipes, photos, videos, and instructional material. See page 53 for outdoor grill instructions.

Cheesy Bread Sticks

These soft and rich bread sticks are great for kids' snacks and with soups, pasta, or dips. You can really change up the flavor by using different cheeses for sprinkling on top.

Makes eight 8-inch bread sticks

1 pound (grapefruit-size portion) lean dough (pages 59–95) or Savory Brioche
    dough (page 107)
2 tablespoons olive oil
2 ounces Parmigiano-Reggiano cheese (or any hard grating cheese), finely grated
Parchment paper or oil for the baking sheet

1. **Prepare and measure** all toppings in advance.

2. **Preheat oven to 375°F.** Prepare a baking sheet with parchment paper or oil. Dust the surface of the refrigerated dough with flour and cut off a 1-pound (grapefruit-size) piece. Dust with more flour and quickly shape it into a ball by stretching the surface of the dough around to the bottom on all four sides, rotating the ball a quarter-turn as you go.

3. **Stretch the bread stick dough:** Flatten the dough with your hands and a rolling pin on a work surface to produce a ¼-inch-thick rectangle. Dust with flour to keep the dough from adhering to the surface. Transfer the dough to a large cutting board.

4. **Add the toppings:** Using a pastry brush, paint one side of the dough with 1 tablespoon olive oil and then sprinkle half the cheese over the

top. Press the cheese into the dough so that it sticks to the oil. Flip the dough over and repeat with the remaining oil and cheese. Using a pizza cutter, cut the dough into eight equal strips. Pick up each strip and twist it twice and lay it on the prepared baking sheet. Repeat with remaining strips, leaving about 1 inch between the twisted bread sticks. If any of the cheese falls off while twisting, sprinkle it over the sticks. Loosely cover the bread sticks with plastic wrap and let sit for 15 minutes.

5. **Place the pan of bread sticks into the oven:** Check for doneness in 20 minutes and turn the bread sticks around in the oven if one side is browning faster than the other. It may take up to 5 minutes more in the oven.

6. Allow to cool slightly, preferably on a wire cooling rack. Serve as a snack, with salads, or dipped in soup.

Visit PizzaIn5.com, where you'll find recipes, photos, videos, and instructional material. See page 53 for outdoor grill instructions.

DESSERT PIZZAS AND OTHER TREATS FROM ENRICHED DOUGH

Challah Dough

This dough is mildly enriched, almost brioche but not quite. We use it to create very unorthodox flatbread challahs, *pullas*, and *tsoureki* that don't require any rest time despite the braid (page 266).

Note that egg-enriched doughs must be baked at lower temperatures to prevent scorching (compared with other flatbreads), but higher temperatures (450°F) are tolerated compared to traditional tall braided loaves, because they finish so quickly in the oven.

Makes enough dough for at least eight ¹/₂-pound flat braids (about 10 inches long) or flatbreads (about 12 inches across). The recipe is easily doubled or halved.

INGREDIENT	VOLUME (U.S.)	WEIGHT (U.S.)	WEIGHT (METRIC)
Lukewarm water (100°F or below)	1¾ cups	14 ounces	400 grams
Granulated yeast[1]	1 tablespoon	0.35 ounce	10 grams
Kosher salt[1]	1–1½ tablespoons	0.63–0.94 ounce	17–25 grams
Eggs, large, lightly beaten	4	—	—
Honey	½ cup	6 ounces	170 grams
Unsalted butter, melted (can substitute margarine or neutral-flavored oil)	½ cup	4 ounces	115 grams
Unbleached all-purpose flour	7 cups	2 pounds, 3 ounces	990 grams

[1]Can decrease to taste (see pages 18 and 20).

1. **Mixing and storing the dough:** Mix the yeast, salt, eggs, honey, and melted butter with the water in a 5-quart bowl, or a lidded (not airtight) food container.

2. Mix in the flour without kneading, using a spoon, a 14-cup capacity food processor (with dough attachment), or a heavy-duty stand mixer (with paddle). If you're not using a machine, you may need to use wet hands to incorporate the last bit of flour.

3. Cover (not airtight), and allow it to rest at room temperature until the dough rises and collapses (or flattens on top), approximately

2 hours. Refrigerate it in a lidded (not airtight) container and use over the next 5 days. Or store the dough for up to 2 weeks in the freezer in ¹⁄₂-pound portions. When using frozen dough, thaw it in the refrigerator overnight before use.

4. **On baking day, roll out or stretch the dough** thin to create Braided Challah, *Pulla*, or *Tsoureki*, or *Pletzl* Flatbread (page 266), or use in the enriched recipe of your choice from this chapter, pages 269–279.

VARIATION: Whole Wheat Flatbread Challah Dough
Substitute 1 cup of whole wheat flour for all-purpose white flour (use either white whole wheat or traditional whole wheat flour). Increase the water to 2 cups, decrease the butter or oil to ¹⁄₃ cup, and decrease to 3 eggs.

Visit PizzaIn5.com, where you'll find recipes, photos, videos, and instructional material. See page 53 for outdoor grill instructions.

Sweet Brioche Dough

This decadent dough is rich with butter and eggs. It makes a perfect dessert when topped with fruit and other sweet toppings.

Makes enough dough for at least eight ¹/₂-pound pizzas or flatbreads. The recipe is easily doubled or halved.

INGREDIENT	VOLUME (U.S.)	WEIGHT (U.S.)	WEIGHT (METRIC)
Lukewarm water	1¼ cups	10 ounces	280 grams
Granulated yeast[1]	1 tablespoon	0.35 ounce	10 grams
Kosher salt[1]	1–1½ tablespoons	0.63–0.94 ounce	17–25 grams
Eggs, large, lightly beaten	5	10 ounces	280 grams
Vanilla	2 teaspoons	—	—
Sugar	1 cup	7 ounces	200 grams
Unbleached all-purpose flour	6½ cups	2 pounds	900 grams
Unsalted butter, melted and slightly cooled	¾ cup (1½ sticks)	6 ounces	175 grams

[1]Can decrease to taste (see pages 18 and 20).

1. **Mixing and storing the dough:** Mix the yeast, salt, eggs, vanilla, and sugar with the water in a 5-quart bowl, or a lidded (not airtight) food container.

2. Add the flour and then pour the melted butter over the top. Mix the dough, without kneading, using a spoon, a 14-cup capacity food processor (with dough attachment), or a heavy-duty stand mixer (with paddle). If you're not using a machine, you may need to use wet hands to incorporate the last bit of flour.

3. Cover (not airtight), and allow it to rest at room temperature until the dough rises and collapses (or flattens on top), approximately 2 hours.

4. The dough will be loose, but will firm up when chilled. Don't try to use it without chilling for at least 3 hours, or until firm. Refrigerate it in a lidded (not airtight) container and use over the next 5 days. Or store the dough for up to 2 weeks in the freezer in $\frac{1}{2}$-pound portions. When using frozen dough, thaw it in the refrigerator overnight before use.

5. **On baking day,** use in the enriched recipe of your choice (pages 269–279).

Visit PizzaIn5.com, where you'll find recipes, photos, videos, and instructional material. See page 53 for outdoor grill instructions.

Chocolate Dough

This dough is sophisticated enough to satisfy adults in need of a chocolate fix, but sweet enough to make the perfect dessert for kids.

Makes enough dough for at least eight ¹/₂-pound dough portions. The recipe is easily doubled or halved.

INGREDIENT	VOLUME (U.S.)	WEIGHT (U.S.)	WEIGHT (METRIC)
Lukewarm water	3¹/₄ cups	1 pound, 10 ounces	740 grams
Granulated yeast[1]	1 tablespoon	0.35 ounce	10 grams
Kosher salt[1]	1–1¹/₂ tablespoons	0.63–0.94 ounce	17–25 grams
Sugar	1 cup	8 ounces	225 grams
Unbleached all-purpose flour	6 cups	1 pound, 14 ounces	840 grams
Cocoa powder (natural or Dutch processed)	1¹/₂ cups	4 ounces	110 grams

[1]Can decrease to taste (see pages 18 and 20).

1. **Mixing and storing the dough:** Mix the yeast, salt, and sugar with the water in a 5-quart bowl, or a lidded (not airtight) food container.

2. Mix in the remaining dry ingredients without kneading, using a spoon, a 14-cup capacity food processor (with dough attachment), or a

heavy-duty stand mixer (with paddle). If you're not using a machine, you may need to use wet hands to incorporate the last bit of flour.

3. Cover (not airtight), and allow it to rest at room temperature until the dough rises and collapses (or flattens on top), approximately 2 hours.

4. The dough can be used immediately after its initial rise, though it is easier to handle when cold. Refrigerate it in a lidded (not airtight) container and use for desserts over the next 7 days. Or store the dough for up to 2 weeks in the freezer in $1/2$-pound portions. When using frozen dough, thaw it in the refrigerator overnight before use.

5. Be careful when baking this dough; the color makes it hard to know when it is fully baked. Check for doneness a couple of minutes early and lift up the edge to make sure it is not overbaking.

6. **On baking day,** use in the enriched recipe of your choice (pages 269–279).

Gluten-Free Sweet Enriched Pizza Dough

Lightly sweet and rich, this dough is perfect for creating any of the dessert pizzas in this chapter. Follow the quick and easy directions below for rolling out this gluten-free dough, then top it with anything from fresh fruit to Chocolate-Banana Cream Pie (page 275).

Makes enough dough for at least eight ¹/₂-pound pizzas or flatbreads (about 12 inches across). The recipe is easily doubled or halved.

INGREDIENT	VOLUME (U.S.)	WEIGHT (U.S.)	WEIGHT (METRIC)
Brown rice flour	1 cup	5½ ounces	160 grams
White rice flour	1 cup	5 ounces	140 grams
Tapioca flour (tapioca starch)	4 cups	1 pound, 1 ounce	500 grams
Granulated yeast	1½ tablespoons	0.55 ounce	15 grams
Kosher salt[1]	1–1½ tablespoons	0.63–0.94 ounce	17–25 grams
Xanthan gum	2 tablespoons	—	—
Lukewarm milk[2]	2 cups	1 pound	455 grams
Honey	1 cup	12 ounces	340 grams
Unsalted butter, melted, slightly cooled[3]	1 cup	8 ounces	230 grams

[1]Can decrease to taste (see page 20). [2]Can substitute soy, rice, or almond milk.
[3]Can use butter substitute.

(continued)

INGREDIENT	VOLUME (U.S.)	WEIGHT (U.S.)	WEIGHT (METRIC)
Eggs, large, lightly beaten (see 97 for substitute)	5	10 ounces	280 grams
Butter or neutral-flavored oil for greasing pan			
Granulated sugar for rolling out dough			

1. **Mixing and storing the dough:** Whisk together the rice flours, tapioca flour (starch), yeast, salt, and xanthan gum in a 5-quart bowl, or a lidded (not airtight) food container.

2. Combine the liquid ingredients and gradually mix them with the dry ingredients, using a spoon, 14-cup food processor (with dough attachment), or a heavy-duty stand mixer (with paddle). If you're not using a machine, you may need to use wet hands to incorporate the last bit of flour.

3. Cover (not airtight), and allow it to rest at room temperature until the dough rises, approximately 2 hours.

4. The dough will be loose, but will firm up when chilled. Don't try to use it without chilling for at least 3 hours, or until firm. Refrigerate it in a lidded (not airtight) container and use over the next 5 days. Or store the dough for up to 2 weeks in the freezer in $1/2$-pound portions. When using frozen dough, thaw it in the refrigerator overnight before use.

5. **On baking day, prepare and measure** all toppings in advance.

6. **Preheat the oven to 350°F.** Lightly grease a nonstick silicone mat or parchment paper with butter or oil. Using wet hands, tear off a ½-pound (orange-size) piece. Quickly shape it into a ball; this dough isn't stretched because there is no gluten in it—just gently press it into the shape of a ball.

7. **Flatten the dough** with your hands onto the greased surface. Dust the top of the dough with granulated sugar, and cover with plastic wrap. Use a rolling pin to produce a ¹⁄₁₆-inch-thick round, dusting with more sugar to keep the dough from sticking to the plastic.

8. **Add the toppings:** Follow the directions for any of our dessert pizzas to top and bake the dough.

Almond Cream

This almond-flavored topping is the perfect match for many of our fruit desserts.

Makes 1 cup almond cream. The recipe is easily doubled or halved.

$^1/_2$ cup (4 ounces) almond paste

4 tablespoons ($^1/_2$ stick) unsalted butter

2 tablespoons sugar

1 large egg yolk

1 tablespoon all-purpose flour (rice flour for gluten-free)

$^1/_4$ teaspoon almond extract

1. Mix all the ingredients in a stand mixer or food processor until smooth.

2. Store in the refrigerator for up to 5 days or freeze for later use.

Vanilla Pastry Cream

This rich vanilla custard is wonderful spread thin and topped with any seasonal fruit for a breakfast or dessert pizza. It is even more indulgent layered with chocolate (see Boston Cream Pie, page 276).

Makes 2 cups pastry cream. The recipe is easily doubled or halved.

3 tablespoons cornstarch
$1/2$ cup sugar
1 large egg
3 large egg yolks
2 cups milk
2 tablespoons unsalted butter
Pinch of salt
$1/2$ vanilla bean, scraped, or 1 teaspoon pure vanilla extract

1. Whisk together the cornstarch and $1/4$ cup of the sugar. Add egg and egg yolks and mix into a smooth paste, set aside.

2. Bring the milk, remaining $1/4$ cup of sugar, butter, salt, and vanilla bean to a gentle boil in a medium-large saucepan.

3. Slowly, and in small amounts, whisk the hot milk mixture into the egg mixture. Once the egg mixture is warm to the touch, pour it back into the pot.

4. Return the custard to the stovetop and bring to a boil over medium heat, whisking continuously for 3 minutes, until thick and glossy. In

order to properly cook the cornstarch in the custard you need to cook the pastry cream for the full 3 minutes.

5. Transfer to a shallow container and cover with plastic wrap, placed directly on the surface of the pastry cream.

6. Chill in the refrigerator for at least 30 minutes. The pastry cream can be stored for up to 5 days.

Chocolate Ganache

For the craving that only pure chocolate will satisfy. For a more intense flavor, try bittersweet chocolate or go with semisweet if you are looking for something a bit sweeter.

Makes 1¼ cups ganache. The recipe is easily doubled or halved.

¾ cup heavy (whipping) cream
4 ounces bittersweet or semisweet chocolate, finely chopped
1 tablespoon unsalted butter

1. Heat the cream in a medium saucepan over low heat. Once the cream comes to a low simmer, turn off the heat and add the chocolate and butter. Swirl the chocolate in the pot and let sit for 3 minutes before gently whisking together. Be sure there are no lumps.

2. Cover and store in the refrigerator for up to 5 days.

Lemon Curd

Tangy and sweet, this makes a great dessert when paired with fresh fruit or all on its own baked on a sweet brioche crust.

Makes 1½ cups curd. The recipe is easily doubled or halved.

6 large egg yolks
1 cup sugar
½ cup fresh lemon juice
Pinch of salt
1 tablespoon lemon zest
½ cup (1 stick) unsalted butter, cut into 1-inch chunks

1. Whisk together all the ingredients, except the butter, in a large metal bowl.

2. Place the bowl over a pot of gently simmering water, setting up as a double boiler.

3. Stir constantly with a rubber spatula until the lemon curd begins to thicken, about 10 minutes.

4. Add the butter and continue to stir until it is completely melted and the curd is quite thick; it will be the consistency of smooth pudding. If there are any lumps, strain the curd through a fine-mesh sieve. Cover with plastic wrap placed directly on the surface of the lemon curd.

5. Chill in the refrigerator for at least 30 minutes. The curd can be stored for up to 5 days.

Visit PizzaIn5.com, where you'll find recipes, photos, videos, and instructional material. See page 53 for outdoor grill instructions.

Braided *Challah, Pulla, Tsoureki,* or *Pletzl* Flatbread

This is a very quick way to make traditional braided breads like Jewish Sabbath bread (*challah*), Finnish *pulla* (Christmas bread), or Greek *tsoureki* (Easter bread)—but in a fraction of the time. How do we accomplish that? With a very unusual flat-surface braiding technique. Because these braids are done as flatbreads, they don't require any resting, which means braided bread on the spur of the moment becomes a delicious possibility.

"My friend Lisa's grandmother (Yiayia) came from Greece, so Lisa's mom has fond memories of tsoureki *that was eagerly awaited twice a year, not just at Easter. At New Year's, Yiayia baked a good-luck coin into it, and at Easter she twisted some dough into an Orthodox cross (two strands of equal length) and put it on top, with a red Easter egg at the center."*—Jeff

Makes 1 braided flatbread to serve 4

$^1/_2$ pound (orange-size portion) enriched dough (pages 107, 251, or 254)
Oil, butter, or parchment paper for the baking sheet
Egg wash (1 egg beaten with 1 tablespoon water)
Poppy seeds, sesame seeds, or raw sugar for sprinkling

1. **Preheat a baking stone to 425°F for 30 minutes,** on a rack placed near the center of the oven. If you're not using a stone in the oven, a 5-minute preheat is adequate. Prepare a baking sheet with oil, butter, or parchment paper.

2. Dust the surface of the refrigerated dough with flour and cut off a $^1/_2$-pound (orange-size) piece. Dust with more flour and quickly shape

it into a ball by stretching the surface of the dough around to the bottom on all four sides, rotating the ball a quarter-turn as you go.

3. **Flatten the dough** with your hands and a rolling pin on the work surface or directly onto a wooden pizza peel (or shape the disk by hand, see page 42) to produce an elongated 1/8-inch-thick rectangle, dusting with flour to keep the dough from adhering to the board. Use a dough scraper to unstick the dough as needed. When you're done, the dough round should have enough flour under it to move easily when you shake the peel.

4. **Cut the rectangle the long way into three long strips,** using a pizza wheel or a sharp knife, and lay them next to one another on a floured work surface.

5. **Gently coax the strips into a braid,** keeping the strips flat on the table; don't twist them and don't apply tension to the strands. Starting at one end, pull an outer strand over the center strand and lay it down. As you work, you'll always be pulling and alternating outer strands into the middle, never moving what becomes

Visit PizzaIn5.com, where you'll find recipes, photos, videos, and instructional material. See page 53 for outdoor grill instructions.

the center strand. When you get to the end, pinch the strands together but try to keep them flat.

6. Place the braid on the prepared baking sheet. No rest time is needed before baking.

7. Use a pastry brush to paint the top crust with egg wash and then sprinkle with poppy or sesame seeds.

8. **Place the baking sheet in the oven** and bake for about 25 minutes, or until golden brown.

9. Allow the challah to cool on a rack slightly before slicing and eating.

VARIATION: *Pulla*
Add 1 teaspoon ground cardamom and ½ teaspoon ground aniseed to the wet ingredients in the challah dough (page 251). Roll out, cut strips, and braid as above. Paint it with egg wash, but sprinkle it with raw sugar instead of poppy or sesame seeds and bake at 425°F as above.

VARIATION: *Tsoureki* (Greek Easter Bread)
Roll out as a ¾-inch-thick flat round instead of a braid, with a cross of dough made from thin dough-ropes on top. Attach the cross by painting the top with egg wash before laying the cross into place. If you like, place a red-dyed, hard-boiled egg at the center of the cross—press it into place before baking. Finish with sesame seeds.

VARIATION: Onion *Pletzl*
Roll out the dough to ⅛-inch thickness but skip the strip-making and braiding. Lightly scatter barely browned sautéed sliced onions over the dough, sprinkle with poppy seeds, and bake as above.

Fruit Galettes

A lovely breakfast pastry or rustic dessert; these simple individual pizzas are inspired by a sophisticated French tart, but are much faster to make.

Makes eight 4-inch galettes

1 pound (grapefruit-size portion) enriched dough (pages 251–258)
Butter or parchment paper for cookie sheet
1 cup lemon curd (page 265)
1 cup fresh or frozen blueberries
$^1/_2$ cup blueberry preserves
Egg wash (1 egg beaten with 1 tablespoon water)
Sugar for sprinkling

1. **Prepare and measure** all toppings in advance. Prepare two baking sheets with butter or parchment paper.

2. **Preheat the oven to 350°F,** with racks in the center and top third of the oven.

3. Dust the surface of the refrigerated dough with flour and cut off a 1-pound (grapefruit-size) piece. Dust with more flour and quickly shape it into a ball by stretching the surface of the dough around to the bottom on all four sides, rotating the ball a quarter-turn as you go. Divide the ball into 8 equal portions and roll the small pieces into balls.

4. **Roll out the galettes:** Flatten the dough with your hands and a rolling pin on a work surface to produce a $^1/_8$-inch-thick round. Dust with

flour to keep the dough from adhering to the surface. Use a dough scraper to unstick the dough as needed. Continue with the other pieces. Transfer the circles to the prepared baking sheets.

5. **Add the toppings:** Distribute 2 tablespoons of the lemon curd in the center of each of the 8 circles, then add the blueberries and preserves, keeping all the fillings toward the center of the dough. Brush the edge of the dough very lightly with egg wash. Crimp the edges. Once they are all crimped, paint the edges with more egg wash and sprinkle with sugar.

6. **Slide the pans into the preheated oven.** Check for browning in 8 to 10 minutes and switch the sheets from the top to bottom rack to ensure that they bake evenly. Continue to bake for 8 to 10 minutes more, or until the edges are golden and the filling is bubbling.

7. Allow to cool slightly, preferably on a wire cooling rack. The galettes can be served warm or at room temperature.

VARIATIONS: Replace the lemon curd, blueberries, and preserves with:

Cherry
1 cup almond cream (page 261)
$1^1\!/2$ cups fresh or frozen pitted sour cherries
$^1\!/2$ cup cherry preserves

Raspberry
1 cup pastry cream (page 262)
1 cup fresh or frozen raspberries
$^1\!/2$ cup raspberry preserves

Chocolate-Raspberry

Use chocolate dough (page 256)

1 cup chocolate ganache (page 264)

1 cup fresh or frozen raspberries

1/2 cup raspberry preserves

Apple-Pear

1 cup almond cream (page 261)

1 apple, thinly sliced

1 pear, thinly sliced

1 teaspoon ground cinnamon

2 teaspoons sugar

Toss the apple and pear slices with the cinnamon and sugar in a bowl. Fill the galettes with 2 tablespoons of almond cream and distribute the apple-pear filling evenly over the top before baking.

Blush Apple Tart

We chose an apple with a red skin and tart flesh for this gorgeous pizza. The sweetness of the brioche dough and raspberry preserves is a perfect balance for the tartness of the apples. If you can't find a red-skinned apple that fits the bill, then Granny Smith will do the trick, but you will want to peel them first to create the blushed look of the baked tart.

Makes one 12-inch tart

$1/2$ pound (orange-size portion) enriched dough (pages 251 or 254), or Gluten-Free Sweet Enriched Pizza Dough (page 258)
Butter for the baking sheet
$1/4$ cup applesauce or almond cream (page 261)
2 tablespoons raspberry preserves
2 unpeeled tart red apples, washed, sliced very thin, preferably on a mandoline (see sidebar, page 136)
2 tablespoons sugar for sprinkling

1. **Preheat the oven to 350°F.** Grease a baking sheet with butter.

2. Combine the applesauce (or almond cream) and raspberry preserves in a small bowl.

3. Dust the surface of the refrigerated dough with flour and cut off a $1/2$-pound (orange-size) piece. Dust with more flour and quickly shape it into a ball by stretching the surface of the dough around to the bottom on all four sides, rotating the ball a quarter-turn as you go.

4. **Stretch the tart crust:** Flatten the dough with your hands and a rolling pin on a work surface to produce a $1/8$-inch-thick round. Dust with flour to keep the dough from adhering to the surface. Use a dough scraper to unstick the dough as needed. Transfer the dough to the prepared baking sheet.

5. **Add the toppings:** Spread the applesauce mixture evenly over the dough, going nearly to the edge. Arrange the apples in concentric circles, starting at the outside edge. Sprinkle with sugar.

APPLES

Across the country there are incredible varieties of apples to bake with. Some of our favor for this tart and the other apple recipes are: Cortland, Jonathan, Honey Crisp, Ida Red, and Winesap. You can also use a combination of the apples to get a more interesting flavor. All of them keep their shape while baking, which makes for a gorgeous tart.

6. **Slide the baking sheet into the oven:** Check for doneness in 20 minutes; at this time, turn the pizza around in the oven if one side is browning faster than the other. It may take up to 5 minutes more in the oven.

7. Allow to cool slightly, preferably on a wire cooling rack. Cut into wedges and serve.

Visit PizzaIn5.com, where you'll find recipes, photos, videos, and instructional material. See page 53 for outdoor grill instructions.

Banana Cream Hand Pie

Here's an old-fashioned diner classic made new again as individual hand pies. We take a spoon of homemade vanilla pudding, a stack of banana slices, and a sprinkle of graham crackers and wrap them all up in sweet dough. It is meant for dessert, but quick and easy enough for an afternoon snack. For a party, it's fun to make the pies with a variety of fillings such as chocolate ganache, lemon curd, and coconut cream (see variations below).

Makes eight 3-inch pies

1 pound (grapefruit-size portion) enriched dough (pages 251–258)
$1/2$ cup Vanilla Pastry Cream (page 262)
$1/2$ cup crushed graham crackers
2 bananas
Butter or parchment paper for the baking sheets
Egg wash (1 egg beaten with tablespoon water)
Sugar for sprinkling

1. **On baking day, prepare and measure** all toppings in advance. Prepare two baking sheets with butter or parchment paper.

2. **Preheat the oven to 350°F,** with racks in the center and top third of the oven.

3. Dust the surface of the refrigerated dough with flour and cut off a 1-pound (grapefruit-size) piece. Dust with more flour and quickly shape it into a ball by stretching the surface of the dough around to the bottom on all four sides, rotating the ball a quarter-turn as you go.

4. **Roll out the dough:** Flatten the dough with your hands and a rolling pin on a work surface to produce a $\frac{1}{8}$-inch-thick rectangle. Dust with flour to keep the dough from adhering to the surface. Use a dough scraper to unstick the dough as needed.

5. **Cut the dough into 8 equal square pieces by making 3 cuts along the long end of the dough,** using a pastry wheel or pizza cutter, then cutting those in half from the short end.

6. **Add the toppings:** Spoon 1 tablespoon of the pastry cream into the center of each piece of dough. Cover the pastry cream with 1 tablespoon crushed graham crackers and 2 or 3 slices of banana. Using a pastry brush, paint the edge of the dough with egg wash. Fold the dough over the filling to connect the points, which will form a triangle. Pinch the edges together so the filling will not escape while baking. Arrange the triangles on the prepared sheets so they have plenty of room to rise in the oven. Brush the tops with more egg wash and sprinkle with sugar.

7. **Slide the baking sheets into the oven on the middle rack.** Check for doneness in 18 to 20 minutes and turn the pan around in the oven if one side is browning faster than the other. It may take up to 5 minutes more in the oven.

8. Allow to cool slightly, preferably on a wire cooling rack. Serve as an afternoon snack or a fun brunch dessert.

VARIATION: Chocolate-Banana Cream Pie

Add 1 teaspoon of Chocolate Ganache (page 264) over the pastry cream and banana slices before folding the dough. Follow the baking instructions above.

VARIATION: Coconut Cream Pie
Replace the bananas with $1/2$ cup shredded coconut. Mix the coconut with the pastry cream and fill each of the dough pieces with 3 tablespoons of the filling. Omit the graham crackers. Follow the baking instructions above.

VARIATION: Boston Cream Pie
Replace the bananas and graham crackers with 1 additional tablespoon pastry cream and 1 tablespoon Chocolate Ganache (page 264). Follow the baking instructions above. When the pies come from the oven let them cool and glaze the top with more of the ganache.

VARIATION: Lemon Pie
Replace the bananas and graham crackers with 2 tablespoons lemon curd (page 265) over the pastry cream. Follow the baking instructions above. Allow the pies to cool and drizzle on lemon icing ($1/2$ cup confectioners' sugar mixed with 1 tablespoon fresh lemon juice and 1 tablespoon heavy cream).

Skillet Apple Pie

As good as grandma's apple pie, but faster! A thin crust of sweet brioche filled with brown sugar, cinnamon, and tart apples is topped with streusel and baked in a skillet. It makes a perfect breakfast or a dessert served à la mode. Try the peach variation in the summertime.

Makes one 12-inch pie

¾ pound (large orange-size portion) enriched dough (pages 251–258)

3 teaspoons unsalted butter, for the skillet and brushing on the top crust

1 tablespoon sugar for sprinkling over top crust

Streusel Topping

¼ cup old-fashioned rolled oats

¼ cup all-purpose flour

¼ teaspoon salt

½ teaspoon ground cinnamon

¼ cup brown sugar, well packed

¼ cup unsalted butter, melted

Filling

4 large Granny Smith apples, peeled, cored, thinly sliced, preferably on a mandoline (see sidebar, page 136)

½ cup brown sugar, firmly packed

½ teaspoon ground cinnamon

1 tablespoon all-purpose flour

1 teaspoon lemon zest

Visit PizzaIn5.com, where you'll find recipes, photos, videos, and instructional material. See page 53 for outdoor grill instructions.

1. **Make the streusel topping:** In a medium bowl, blend together the oats, flour, salt, cinnamon, brown sugar, and melted butter. Set aside.

2. **Prepare the fruit filling:** In a large bowl combine the apples, brown sugar, cinnamon, flour, and zest.

3. **Preheat the oven to 350°F.** Coat the bottom of a 10-inch ovenproof skillet with 2 teaspoons butter. Dust the surface of the refrigerated dough with flour and cut off a ¾-pound (large orange-size) piece. Dust with more flour and quickly shape it into a ball by stretching the surface of the dough around to the bottom on all four sides, rotating the ball a quarter-turn as you go.

4. **Roll out the dough:** Flatten the dough with your hands and a rolling pin on a work surface to produce a ¼-inch-thick circle. Dust with flour to keep the dough from adhering to the surface. Use a dough scraper to unstick the dough as needed.

5. Drape the dough into the prepared skillet, making sure that the dough comes all the way up the sides of the pan.

6. **Add the apples and topping:** Fill the brioche with the apple filling and then cover with the streusel topping. Flop the dough that is overhanging the pan over the filling. Brush this dough with remaining butter and sprinkle with sugar.

7. **Slide the skillet into the oven on the bottom rack.** Check for doneness in 45 to 60 minutes by poking

the apples with a knife to see if they are tender. If the dough along the edge is getting too brown, drape the skillet loosely with foil.

8. Allow to cool slightly, preferably on a wire cooling rack, cut into wedges, and serve with your favorite ice cream.

VARIATION: Skillet Peach Pie
Replace the apples with peaches, and add $1/8$ teaspoon ground ginger to the filling. For the streusel topping, use ground ginger in place of the cinnamon.

Visit PizzaIn5.com, where you'll find recipes, photos, videos, and instructional material. See page 53 for outdoor grill instructions.

SOURCES FOR BAKING PRODUCTS

Bob's Red Mill: www.bobsredmill.com, 800-349-2173

The Chef's Gallery (Stillwater, Minnesota): www.thechefsgallery.com, 651-351-1144

Cooks of Crocus Hill (St. Paul and Edina, Minnesota): www.cooksofcrocushill.com, 651-228-1333 or 952-285-1903

Emile Henry USA: www.EmileHenryUSA.com, 888-346-8853

Hodgson Mill: www.hodgsonmill.com, 800-347-0105

King Arthur Flour: www.kingarthurflour.com/shop/, 800-827-6836

Lodge Cast Iron cookware: www.lodgemfg.com, 423-837-7181

Penzeys Spices: www.penzeys.com, 800-741-7787

Red Star Yeast: www.redstaryeast.com, 800-445-4746

Tupperware: www.tupperware.com, 800-366-3800

SOURCES CONSULTED

Athenaeus. *The Deipnosophists*. London: William Heinemann Ltd., 1927.

Grant, Mark. *Roman Cookery*. London: Serif, 1999.

Langton, Brenda. *The Cafe Brenda Cookbook*: Seafood and Vegetarian Cuisine. Minneapolis: University of Minnesota Press, 2004.

Ministry of Agriculture, Department of Agricultural Food Product Quality and Consumer Protection, *Repubblica Italiana. Summary: Proposal for Recognition of the Specialità Tradizionale Garantita "Pizza Napoletana."* May 24, 2004.

U.S. Department of Agriculture Fact Sheet. *Egg Products Preparation: Shell Eggs from Farm to Table.* http://www.fsis.usda.gov/fact_sheets/focus_on_shell _eggs/index.asp, accessed May 1, 2011.

INDEX

Visit PizzaIn5.com, where you'll find recipes, photos, videos, and instructional material. See
page 53 for outdoor grill instructions.

Visit PizzaIn5.com, where you'll find recipes, photos, videos, and instructional material. See page 53 for outdoor grill instructions.

Visit PizzaIn5.com, where you'll find recipes, photos, videos, and instructional material. See page 53 for outdoor grill instructions.

Visit PizzaIn5.com, where you'll find recipes, photos, videos, and instructional material. See page 53 for outdoor grill instructions.

Visit PizzaIn5.com, where you'll find recipes, photos, videos, and instructional material. See page 53 for outdoor grill instructions.